An Introd

TRANS

STUDIES

An Introduction to
TRANSPORT STUDIES

3rd Edition

John Hibbs

The Institute of
Logistics and Transport

KOGAN
PAGE

First published in 1970 by John Baker
First published by Kogan Page 1988
This edition published 2000

Kogan Page Limited
120 Pentonville Road
London N1 9JN

The masculine pronoun has been used throughout this book. This stems from a desire to avoid ugly or cumbersome language, and no discrimination, prejudice or bias is intended.

British Library Cataloguing in Publication Data

A CIP record for this book is available from the British Library.

ISBN 0 7494 2946 1

Typeset by JS Typesetting, Wellingborough, Northamptonshire
Printed and bound by Clays Ltd, St Ives plc

Contents

Foreword

There has never been a more appropriate time to study transport or to make transport your chosen career. The publication in the summer of 1998 of the 'New Deal' White Paper provided ample evidence, if it were needed, of the problems being faced by the UK transport network. Given these problems, the future integrity of transport requires policies of a radical, sustainable nature to be promoted, developed and implemented by committed, highly motivated planners, economists, engineers, technologists and managers to ensure that this vitally important sector of industry can fulfil its essential economic and social objectives.

This book is written by a well-known and highly respected 'transportant' – the term used by the former Chartered Institute of Transport to describe the transport professional. Professor John Hibbs is not just an academic who writes about transport – he is a professional academic who bases what he writes on an earlier career in passenger transport management. As an academic John has maintained regular contact with many senior figures in transport. The outcome is a clearly written, authoritative text that leaves the reader in no doubt as to what have been and what will be the key issues in transport.

This book will appeal as a first text to students of transport across all modes of passenger and freight transport. The last two chapters will be of particular relevance to aspiring transportants. These provide a clear insight into the skills and qualities needed for a successful career in transport and the education and training possibilities.

From a personal standpoint, the 1970 edition of *An Introduction to Transport Studies* was the first transport text I read. At the time it gave me considerable encouragement to find out more about this fascinating industry, one in which I too have made my career. It is my sincere hope that this third edition will do the same for its readers.

Professor Colin G Bamford
University of Huddersfield

Introduction

Society as it exists in cities throughout the world is entirely dependent upon three industries: agriculture, public health and transport. The importance of the first is plain, while the second, which includes sewerage and refuse disposal as well as clean water, can do more than medicine to maintain a disease-free environment. Yet each of them is dependent upon the efficient movement of goods. Cities, and indeed every community above the simplest, rely upon transport to move materials for the manufacture of goods and the provision of services, and for distribution of the 'finished product' to customers. People rely on it to find their way to where they work, and home again. During the period known as the 'Dark Ages' (the fifth to eighth centuries AD) neither travel nor trade was possible, and the growth of modern European civilisation began with the enforcement of conditions of safety.

The transport industry is made up of two parts: the *infra-structure*, and what *moves* on it. Infrastructure includes roads, railway track, seaports and airports, the electricity and gas grids and the water mains and sewers. Telephone and radio form the infrastructure for the conveyance of messages, including the Internet. Cars and buses, trains and lorries, ships and aircraft, and messages, all move over the infrastructure, and if it fails there are serious consequences; a familiar one is the lack of electricity when the cables are down.

But it is the movement industry that we mostly think of when we talk about transport. That is why we speak of 'the movement of goods' or 'the movement of people'. And the efficiency of the industry is of vital importance, for the economy as a whole, and for the businesses that depend upon it.

Business logistics, which is about the efficient management of the 'supply-chain' and of distribution, could not function without reliable transport and information (which we have seen to be a special aspect of transport). It includes many other activities, such as purchasing, packaging, advertising and cost accounting, but without transport it would have no function. Transport is equally essential for **tourism**, which is the fastest growing industry in the modern world. Yet tourism is also dependent upon efficient logistics, in the movement of people and of the goods necessary for hospitality management.

Decisions about logistics are taken all the time, even when we decide whether or not to get the car out to go to the pictures. But they are made against the background of transport provision, and this means that to study and understand the transport industry must be the prime concern of those who want to see a better future. This does not make the industry unique – just essential. And it means that transport offers you a valuable and highly satisfying career.

John Hibbs
University of Central England
October 1999

1

Why Study Transport?

Confound romance . . . and all unseen
Romance brought up the nine-fifteen

Rudyard Kipling, *The King*

BACKGROUND AND DEVELOPMENTS

We don't expect to find transport as a subject for poetry, but then we don't perhaps read Kipling very often. From his lifetime to ours, transport has been the Cinderella of the basic industries: only recently, here and abroad, has it become a recognised subject for academic study. Shipping and airways are considered to hold a certain romance but the humdrum business of roads and rails, of running buses and lorries and trains – all this has frequently been consigned to the level of plumbing or motor mechanics. It has been seen as a subject for training at technical level, rather than education in order to 'master' it.

With a false romanticism that Kipling would have scorned we deplore the departure of steam, or the growth of containerised shipping, or the substitution of the motor car for the pony and trap. It is easier today to publish glossy magazines for transport enthusiasts than to sustain a serious discussion of the industry in a reputable journal for more than two issues. And yet the idea of higher education in the field of transport studies attracts young men and women from all over the country to those universities and colleges that have courses to offer.

The growing trend to a serious interest in the transport industry no doubt reflects a recognition of its fundamental importance. Was it not Kipling also who remarked 'transport is civilisation'? When, in time of war or economic restraint, we find movement restricted and the necessities as well as the luxuries of life expensive and in short supply, we realise the truth of his words. The empires of the past depended for their existence upon transport.

In the nineteenth century, when the railways began to offer for the first time in history a means of travel accessible to everyone, society was not slow in recognising their benefits. As soon as a train service had been started, the General Post Office transferred the mail to it. Queen Victoria's first journey by train in 1842 gave the seal of public approval to rail travel just as the Admiralty had given approval to the steamship in 1838 by inviting tenders for a mail contract across the Atlantic.

But there were those who opposed both, just as there are those today who oppose the replacement of railways by forms of transport that have in turn won the approval of our age. A cycle has been completed in both inland and international transport; the Railway Age has come to an end, while the aeroplane has all but replaced the ocean liner on regular passenger services.

This cyclical change is both reinforced and complicated by the very basic shift taking place in the optimal use of energy for transport and many other purposes. In a universe awash with energy, this is partly a technological problem which the laws of supply and demand will bear upon to obtain a solution. The geopolitical consequences of over-dependence upon cheap oil can present this problem as a crisis, but the remedies are within reach, even if their consequences for transport are still difficult to discern. Change is inevitable, but the demand for transport, as we have seen, is unlikely to fall so long as civilisation survives. This will ensure that energy is made available in such a form as will continue to satisfy our needs.

Developments in technology have affected the transport industry since the invention of the wheel and the sail, and they will undoubtedly continue to do so. Information Technology (IT) is just the latest of these. Twofold in its effects, it offers more choice to transport users, while at the same time it improves the competitive position of firms in the industry. Governments, too, play their part in the process of change, with which the industry must come to terms. The Trans-European Networks (TENS) being developed by the European Commission treat short sea crossings to and from Great Britain, Ireland, the Mediterranean islands and Scandinavia as if the dividing ocean did not exist – as, for air transport, it does not.

The impact of the aeroplane upon the world's passenger shipping may be compared with that of the motor car upon inland public transport, the principal difference being the greater awareness we all feel of the private car revolution. But it is also true that the growth of car ownership is presenting more problems to society than perhaps any other change in the sphere of travel and transport. The private car offers advantages not generally available by public transport; at the same time its widespread use makes the provision of efficient *public* transport increasingly difficult. The resulting situation seems to undermine the advantages of each.

As long as this conflict is built into the situation the problem will worsen. In many ways this is at the heart of our subject, for it is this very conflict that has driven governments to intervene more and more in the economic and commercial aspects of inland transport. And it is attracting the interests of people to whom, in the past, the industry has appeared unimportant.

The impact of the international container has been as substantial as that of the private car, though in a different way. As often happens, we have here an invention called forth to ease the burden of rising costs which is then seen to have many other advantages. The modern ocean-going or cross-channel ship has become an extremely expensive investment. One of the first principles of transport is that no vessel or vehicle earns anything unless it is moving (a waiting taxi always excepted). The cross-channel ferries have for years been making more and more journeys by way of tighter and tighter schedules, but they can be loaded and unloaded fairly quickly. In the deep sea trades the picture is different. The traditional freight liner required at least a week at the dockside at each end of her voyage to unload cargo and take on new. The problem has been met by the development of the sealed container. The shipowner merely charges for carrying a box, and container ships today are designed just to carry boxes.

The first advantage of containerisation is that it cuts out the need for a ship to lie idle so long while loading and discharging. Instead of waiting at the quayside while cargo arrives in consignments of every size at irregular intervals for a week, the container ship can tie up, offload the boxes that contain her cargo, take on another set of boxes and be gone within 24 hours. More of her life is thus spent at sea. This means more profit for her owner, while the trader whose goods she carries avoids the risk of damage that goes with trans-shipment at each end of the voyage. He can even clear his dues at an inland customs port so that the container remains sealed and unopened from the commencement of its journey by freight-liner to its final delivery to the customer by a US trucking concern in the Midwest. Some container lines operate around the world, picking up and setting down the boxes at key ports in the United States, Europe and the Far East, while other ships provide the links with the rest of the world.

Containers are easier to load, and since their rates reflect the weight and dimensions of the box, the shipowner no longer has to carry empty space for nothing, as he would have to if shipping, say, an uncrated motor car; international standards have been set up for the size of containers and now ships are designed specifically for the purpose of carrying them. New port installations have appeared too, for containers need open space with hard standing while they await loading, whether into the ship or on to the train or lorry. In each case warehouses at the dock side are now out of date. And, as a final consequence, the boundaries between shipping and land transport are becoming confused, with new brokerage firms growing up to handle the problems of getting the goods together in container loads from a variety of shippers, and of adjusting the rates. A similar confusion exists between road and rail, with the further development of the piggyback road wagon that can be carried by train.

All of this has led to the development of a body of practice known as *logistics*, which is concerned with the efficient use of transport in all modes, to avoid what may be called the waste of time in the processes that form part of the supply chain (these include warehousing and stock control). The Institute of Logistics, which is concerned in this field, has now become part of the Institute of Logistics and Transport, and new developments, including the study of 'passenger logistics', are looked forward to.

THE ADVENT OF TRANSPORT STUDIES

Such developments account for the feeling that transport can no longer be left to the experts. It is no longer eccentric to acknowledge an interest in transport, although even now it is probably more acceptable to be an engineer or an economist with a special concern for the industry than it is to be specifically a 'transportant'. Not surprisingly, practical transport operators tend to resent this belated interest in their industry, which may strike them as an unjustified interference. Yet they themselves may be open to some criticism for living in a closed world for so long.

This used to be especially true of the railways. In 1903 the chairman of the Great Western was referring to 'outside persons' who were successfully running motors. The decline of rail transport tended to emphasise the railwayman's feeling of being on his own in a hostile world. But the bus and coach industry, road haulage and shipping all experienced such shifts to some extent, as did the airlines.

A wider interest in the transport industry started with the realisation, inescapable by the end of the 1950s, that the finances of British Railways were such as to give serious concern to the government. This led to the radical restructuring of the nationalised transport undertakings, under the Transport Act of 1962. The Treasury then took the lead in re-thinking the status of the nationalised corporations, whose lack of financial control was a source of serious concern. Then, with the return of a Labour government in 1964, and the appointment of Barbara Castle as Minister of Transport in December 1965, the objective of a unified policy for public and private transport came to the fore.

Between 1966 and 1968 a series of White Papers appeared on aspects of transport policy that deserve careful reading still. From these the Transport Act of 1968 evolved, which freed the road freight transport industry of many constraints on its operations, and at the same time imposed new ones on the road passenger side. Transport policy then became a matter of party politics, in which it seemed that transportants were given little say. That the debate was not always well-informed followed from the uncertainty of the professionals as to their status, as well as the lack of any objective study of the industry. Books appearing at this time tended to take preconceived positions as to the nature of the industry and the desirable objectives of policy. This, while part of the democratic political process, naturally tended to annoy those who could speak from experience. Yet there were few who seemed ready to break out of their old closed world. The first academic periodical, *The Journal of Transport Economics & Policy*, commenced publication only in 1967. It has been emulated by others since.

The wider interest in the industry ought to be welcomed. By the end of the century its status in public debate had been much improved. The starting point for this book echoes the conviction of the founding fathers of the Chartered Institute of Transport, voiced at its formation (as the Institute of Transport) in 1919, that there are discernible principles that apply to all modes. The study of the industry must therefore be multi-modal. The status of transport as an activity is enhanced by the extent to which it is seen as a unified industry, even though its components engage in competition that is itself a constructive force. One clear indication that the industry had come of age was the royal patronage accorded to its senior professional body, and especially the active interest in the affairs of the Chartered Institute taken by HRH the Princess Royal as its Honorary President.

2

The Approaches to Transport

Oh the after-tram-ride quiet . . .

John Betjeman, *Parliament Hill Fields*

HISTORY, TRADITION AND 'FLAIR'

For those who remember the British variety of electric tramway, Betjeman's description of a journey to Highgate recalls the flavour of a form of transport now virtually abandoned. For some, such nostalgia may seem remote from the serious study of an important industry. Indeed, self-indulgent nostalgia can impede progress more readily than anything else. But management, if it is to be effective, needs a quality commonly called flair. While it is not easily taught, it needs to be present in any adequate transportant. In the present, flair is a near equivalent of the feeling for the past that Betjeman's nostalgia evokes in us.

The study of transport history has progressed vastly since the Second World War, and the importance of historical studies as a means of understanding the structure of the industry is increasingly recognised. But the historical approach can do

10

more than show us how things came to be as they are; it can help us to understand this intangible element we call flair, and to see where its significance lies. For the possessor of true flair is the one who understands instinctively the traditions, and who knows without thinking when and where to ignore or modify them.

We are faced here with the need to recognise the lines of division that run through the transport industry. Each mode has its own history and its own tradition. Indeed, the concept of transport as a unified industry is a relatively new one: until 1914 inland transport meant railways and international transport meant shipping. Now road transport has established itself long enough to have its own traditions. The fact that these are bound up with its successful struggle with the railways makes them a divisive factor. The same is true in the air, where the new industry has grown in part by the transfer of passengers and freight from the older modes of transport.

However regrettable these divisions may seem, in a historical sense they are inescapable. The idea of a unified industry, managed by some hardly imaginable genius who could harmonise the different functions of the different modes and provide exactly the transport service each customer required, is no longer seen to be a possibility, and has ceased to be pursued by public policy. Even were some computerised system able to analyse all the data that would be required and present it for decision, the cost of assembling that data (to say nothing of weaknesses inherent in collecting it) would make the exercise impracticable. The contrasting argument, that would trust the forces of competition alone to satisfy the demand for transport, in so far as the customer was prepared to pay, has never been compatible with a road system provided by general taxation. In any case there is a strong argument for imposing a constraint upon the industry in the interests of public safety and amenity. The trend of thought today seems to encourage the different modes to develop their potential usefulness in a spirit of restrained competition.

This is perhaps inescapable, for experience has shown that the management of the railways is more than enough for most people; while the road transport industry deliberately retained a large measure of local autonomy in its structure. Pride and loyalty are proper virtues to be associated with the places where we work, and they make for a better quality of service, but it is hard to take pride in a large and remote organisation. Robert Graves has reminded us[1] that it is regimental pride even more than patriotism that maintains a fighting unit's survival when losses are running at nine men out of ten. The principle applies to industry as well, and staff pride is of a similar order. For a 'busman' – whether a driver or a senior manager – there is loyalty to the firm, to the bus industry, and (for some at least) to transport as a whole.

Thus the individual traditions and the history of each mode of transport are of the greatest importance if we are to understand the industry, and no good can come of ignoring them. Oldest of all are those of the shipping industry. It is these that are changing most today, just as they have had to change most frequently in the past – from sail to steam; from the days when skippers were responsible for finding cargo to the control of the electric telegraph; and now the change from all the old methods to the idea of a ship as a floating platform for containers controlled by computers for the most part, and kept at sea as continuously as possible. It is not surprising that some shipping men sigh for the good old days, but the flair for shipping is seeing to it that the industry adapts to the changing world.

The railways, on the other hand, have had fewer changes to face in a far shorter life. And yet their ability to survive today is dependent upon coming to terms with a change that many railwaymen failed for too long to realise was upon them. For the first hundred years of their existence, railways in Britain had things increasingly their own way. They came to dominate internal transport so effectively as to attain a monopoly position. It was this monopoly that the commercial motor vehicle began to challenge after 1896, and it was the General Strike of 1926 that showed, to all who could see, that the days of railway monopoly were ended forever. That the railways continued to shoulder the responsibilities and constraints that

belong to a great public utility is only partially the responsibility of successive governments that continued to assume the
need for their retention as a total system; this philosophy
dominated the minds of railwaymen for more than another 30
years.

Road transport is so young that people sometimes think it
has no history, and assume (less forgivably) that it has no
traditions. In fact its roots lie further back than those of the
railways, and the modern express coach system has recognisable links with the stagecoach system of pre-railway days.
The country carrier and the tramway have contributed equally
to the motor bus industry of today, while the road haulage
industry retains the names of Pickford and others who were
in business before the railway system came. Air transport, with
the shortest history of all, has developed traditions of its own
that are nonetheless deeply felt, and has perhaps the strongest
esprit de corps of all the transport modes.

TRANSPORT AND SOCIETY AT LARGE

Young people entering the transport industry generally hold
clear views as to which mode they prefer, and often have a
firm grasp of its traditions. Indeed, the instinctive ability to
understand the 'inwardness' of railway operation is often the
first thing that marks the future transport manager. Of course
it does not always follow that young people with this gift make
a career out of it, but it is this type of interest that distinguishes
the potential transport manager from the 'number-taker' whose
interest will soon evaporate.

Not every child feels the fascination of transport to the extent
of wanting to become an engine driver, but this fascination does
seem to extend to a large proportion of the adult world.
Certainly the experience of the railways in rationalising their
system led to opposition that was not always rational on the
part of those who opposed rail closures. For success in transport
it is necessary for the emotions to be involved since they
contribute a great deal to what we have called flair, but what

is remarkable is the *amount* of emotional involvement displayed by the man in the street when transport (and especially rail transport) is the subject of debate.

On the other hand the professional who feels that the amateur is trying to tell him how to do his job responds with a not unnatural feeling of hostility. It is this that gives rise to the slightly ambivalent relationships between the industry and the various organisations of 'enthusiasts' that have grown up around it (some of them now of long standing, and many of them including serious students of the industry, of all ages). But the industry in general realises the value of such societies, especially since their members share the same fascination that has produced the professional, and since they probably assist with recruitment.

It is in the relationship with the 'layman' proper that the industry is sometimes unsure of itself, though it is the business of the public relations branch to promote greater understanding between the two sides. Transportants sometimes seem slow to realise that the product is competitive with all the other things people can spend their money on, and that a take-it-or-leave-it attitude which may have been practical on the part of the railways in their monopoly days is suicide for transport today. The passenger can choose to go by a different mode in many cases and increasingly has the option of using a private car. The trader, too, faced with high freight charges, may decide to move his premises or to sell in a different market, and so reduce his transport costs to a minimum. Such decisions are not always the result of an objective study of costs and benefits; more often than not an element of prejudice enters into them. It is this the industry has constantly to try to overcome.

Unfortunately, the industry is not itself wholly free from prejudice. Transportants tend to live in a closed world. Perhaps the very nature of their responsibility for the safety of large numbers of people makes them acquire a paternalistic attitude, arguing 'we know best' with what appears to be a closed mind. Certainly this is more true the greater the degree of monopoly. Urban transport, railways and air corporations have all come in for criticism on this account.

When you read about transport in newspapers and magazines, or hear it discussed on the radio or television, you must wonder why so little seems to be understood by commentators outside the industry. This is a matter for concern, and it is even more worrying if it appears that the industry itself has taken too little interest in the world outside its doors. No good purpose is served by hiding the facts – or the problems – that transport management is concerned with.

Thus the general interest in transport to be found in many who are not involved in its provision offers a chance of bridging the gap between professional and layman. This is another reason why the greater interest and prestige of transport studies is to be welcomed. No industry as vital to society as this can expect to be left to function in a void. The more it is understood the better it will be able to secure its own aims and prosperity.

THE PROFESSIONAL VIEW

There is another side to the relationship between transport and society. The study of transport may be carried on for its own sake, but it can also be appoached through a number of other disciplines, each of them with something of value to contribute. Among such approaches are those of engineering, finance, geography, economics, law, and town and country planning, each with an interest in both the current management and the historical aspects of transport.

Engineers

The engineers' contribution to the transport industry is of inescapable importance, whether we consider the growth of the railways in the past or the technologies now being developed for the future. The complexity of modern transport systems means that the engineering disciplines are vital to their function. Kipling, in *M'Andrew's Hymn*, described the private world of the engineer, whether in a ship or any other vessel or vehicle. And if the ship's chief engineer was traditionally a man apart, given no more than a word of thanks in passing at the end of the voyage, how much more incognito is the engineer in the railway, the airline or the coach business, who is never seen by the passengers at all.

Yet to view engineering as a separate branch of the transport industry with no links to other departments is dangerous. Over one hundred years ago, Brunel realised that the disadvantage of the steamship in trade was the amount of hull space required to hold her fuel and machinery. He calculated, with impeccable logic, that to increase the size of the hull would not require a proportionate increase in this part of the ship. In the *Great Eastern* he designed a vessel with twice the passenger capacity of the *Queen Mary*, that would carry the whole of the trade between England and the East. Because of trouble over her construction, and especially launching, her owners were bankrupt before the *Leviathan* (as she was eventually christened) was ready to sail, and she was never used for the purpose intended. But surely someone should have asked whether commercial considerations would permit the trade of the East to be carried in one ship, allowing for the interval that must elapse between successive departures from England to Ceylon? They did not.

To the layman, it must seem that any engineering development should be applied by some iron law to the improvement of his condition, but this does not by any means follow. In the early days of railways, there were many who argued that the power of steam would be better applied to road transport, and it was less the relative efficiency of the steam railway than the opposition of vested interest that turned the stream of invention and investment away from the roads. In 1909 the London General Omnibus Company decided to standardise on a petrol rather than a steam bus, even though Clarkson's paraffin-fired steamers gave their passengers a better ride.

Then again, it is often assumed that the longest lasting machines are the most economical, and the engineer quite properly has no wish to construct anything less than the best. Yet the electric tramcar, solidly Edwardian, remained viable in an engineering sense long after it had been made obsolete by the newer motor bus. If trams had *not* been built to last, but had been replaced more frequently, they might have had a better chance of remaining up to date, and might not have acquired the bad name they eventually had with the travelling public.

It is considerations of this kind that must be kept in mind when we are told of the wonderful inventions that will yet revolutionise transport, The engineer must learn to be prepared for the question 'will it pay?' as well as 'will it work?' Traffic engineering can do much to improve the circulation of traffic in our cities, but could it be that congestion is sometimes a lower price to pay than the wholesale loss of amenity that urban motorways impose?

To answer that question is not easy within the traditional framework of finance and accounting. A new technique of analysis is required to produce an objective estimate of the balance of cost and benefit, allowing for values that are no less real for being difficult or impossible to express in numerical terms. We shall return to this when we consider the contribution of economics and law to transport studies, but since cost/benefit calculations are in the last resort financial, and generally relate to proposed investment, they are equally the concern of the finance department.

Financial managers

The idea of finance as a department of management indicates how far the subject has come from the days of plain accounting. Partly this is the result of increased size in all kinds of industrial enterprise, with the development of corporate planning to take the place of the individual entrepreneur. In this sense, financial management is concerned with risk-taking, which is the essence of business. The entrepreneur, risking his own money, can afford to depend upon his own judgement, while the manager, who is responsible to others, requires more objective support. (Where the entrepreneur remains, he can benefit from the new techniques of financial management which reduce the area of judgement; while the concept of corporate planning still implies the ultimate use of judgement in taking decisions.)

The growth of financial management has equally been encouraged by the new tools forged by mathematical and statistical science, and by the development of electronic data processing. The new statistical techniques have made forecasting increasingly accurate as a basis for market research, while mathematics has given us techniques which make it possible to choose between different ways of investing capital, with an objective measure of the likely financial return upon each.

Computer processors

All forms of transport share the problem of perishability, which means that the product cannot be stock-piled. There is little margin if you make a mistake in planning and supplying the product. This is why both railway and airline managements have spent so much time and effort developing techniques for costing their activities. Indeed, the lack of interest in traffic costing has been held to account partly for the decline in efficiency of the bus industry in the 35 years after 1950. But the analysis of costs by economists and management accountants has been greatly helped by computer processing, which not only supplies the necessary information (in great quantities), but also enables it to be presented to managers in a form they can use for making decisions.

The potential manager needs to understand the possibilities as well as the limitations of the computer in providing the relevant data, but there is just as great a need to understand the principles of accountancy and economics. That is why the core subjects of a business studies course are so often made the basis of a course in transport studies. And even in a small, family-run coach or haulage firm, 'seat-of-the-pants' management is no longer sufficient, though the experienced manager at this level will already be much more aware of the costing problem, and will have first-hand knowledge of the nature of transport costs.

Computer literacy is certainly a necessity for the management of any kind of transport business. It may not mean the ability to write programs, though it should include keyboard skills and a critical mastery of software. The computer will never take over the responsibility of management, for its function is to provide management with both data and the means to analyse it; eventually, the manager will have to rely on judgement for decisions about the future. The use of the computer narrows the range within which judgements must be used, and reduces the risk of being wrong. After all, business decisions are always about the future, yet the future is always unknown.

Here we are talking about the development of information technology, pioneered by British Railways in the 1960s, to gauge quickly and accurately just what is going on in the business. Electronic ticket equipment can now provide bus managers with the finest detail of the traffic, day by day, in the form of printouts or visual displays. Techniques (often called management by exception) must be learned to instruct the computer to provide only the data significant for decision-making. These techniques depend in turn upon the economics and accountancy that make up, along with management flair, the skills of traffic costing and pricing.

The computer is employed also for the more mundane but essential functions of the business, like stock control, the calculation of wages and salaries, and the whole area of customer accounts and credit control. Its use spreads over into publicity, with desk-top publishing offering a cost-effective method of producing urgently-needed information for the customers in an attractive house style. The airlines pioneered its use for seat reservation, and train and coach operators are now following this up, while it has a very important and sophisticated use for simulation techniques in training. These range from flight-deck mock-ups for pilots to the use of business games for managers. And the development of computer scheduling, although it has taken a long time, makes traffic planning and staff and vehicle allocation no longer the hit-or-miss operation that it once was.

The computer as controller of the actual operation is already in existence, with fully automated train services on Tyneside and in London's Docklands, while automatic piloting has been familiar in aircraft for a good many years. The complete auto- mation of a railway, allowing for preset priorities and feedback of the consequence of delays at various points in the system, is not just a dream. In road transport the on-board computer that constantly updates its advice as to the optimum choice of route, given radio-transmission of information about congestion, is already available; data as to the quality of the coffee at the next motorway service area will doubtless follow.

But the most remarkable use of the computer here has been in distribution, where very high levels of throughput at 'hub' installations can be controlled by very few staff, to give over- night collection and delivery between any pair of places. On shipboard, the computer has made the deck officer's job increasingly one of routine, though always with the threat of the old enemy, the sea. The future holds still more potential, with the return of sails (the computer setting them to the wind), and the navigation of a small fleet of vessels from the computer on the mother ship. And with the introduction of the inter- national standard container, the fully automated port is a logical development – it has already reached the drawing board.

Geographers

The approach to transport studies through geography is clearly a basic one, since it is difficult to understand the industry without understanding the physical features of the world in which it operates. Railways and canals have become part of our landscape, whether in use or in decay; motorways and airfields will follow. But geographers take an interest in the industry that goes beyond its physical aspects, and they have contributed a great deal to our knowledge of the social functions of transport.

The role of air transport is particularly significant for study here. Geography today is rapidly changing and its new tech- niques will have increasing relevance for the transportant of the future.

Economists, lawyers and planners

Economics, law, and town and country planning are subjects that are themselves closely linked. In the sense that they are jointly concerned with the conflict of various interests they are similarly involved with the most fundamental of transport problems. The law is also concerned with the statutory framework within which the transport industry operates, and which expresses the will of the electors as to the ownership and control of transport undertakings of all kinds. While the economic policies of the state are expressed in the laws which parliament enacts, the powers of the planners are equally dependent upon sanction given by statute.

Within their own disciplines, these subjects each have their own relevance to transport. Before the First World War, the economics of transport was regarded as railway economics only, since the railways were largely where problems were seen to exist. By the time the road transport industry had appeared, a number of very able brains had been turned upon 'the problem of the railways', and it was generally thought that the problem had been solved. The irony lies in the fact that the policies that emerged were applied after the First World War as if road transport had never been invented. Even then, few economists took a serious interest in the transport industry, either at home or abroad, so that it is only since 1945 that a new approach has been made to the theory of the subject.

The new thought on the economics of transport has, however, made rapid strides. Symbolic of this development was the establishment of a learned periodical, devoted to transport economics and policy, and the employment by the Department of Transport of a team of economists.

To begin with, economists were chiefly interested in the problems of investment in transport, and the aspect of the science called macro-economics was predominant. This reflected the general acceptance of centralised planning as the solution to 'the transport problem', and led to the development of mathematical models associated with the concept of 'transportation planning', imported from the United States in the

1960s. But other economists who worked on the problems of scale of output cast doubts on the efficiency of the very large undertakings that emerged from this thinking. The emphasis is turning now to the importance of the consumer, and the understanding of the micro-economics of the industry. There is still very little application of the theory of the firm, although the idea of the contestable market has played a great part in the widespread conviction that managers should be free of regulations (other than controls over safety) that limit their freedom to respond to the market, and give them an artificial protection from the real world of risk and judgement.

The transport professional

It has been said that transport is not really suitable for separate study – that it should be seen as the practical application of wider principles. This would mean that a railway engineer should be an engineer first, and a railwayman after that; a shipping manager, one who applies the broader principles of management to shipping. But that would ignore the special quality that attracts people to transport, whether as professionals or amateurs; the fascination that calls forth in many people a corresponding flair. It leaves out of account the special nature of the work, involving long and inconvenient hours, which is such that some special motivation over and above the pecuniary is surely necessary if men and women are to work in the industry at any level.

For many people transport is a calling (and a not ignoble one), and this seems to have been true for many generations – certainly back as far as the stagecoach era. Transport studies would seem therefore to be justified much as medical studies are; a central function upon which light may be cast from a number of 'purer' disciplines, to each of which a special loyalty must be retained. The transport engineer should remain just that; rather than put engineering loyalty above all, it is essential to feel a bond of common loyalty with the transport accountant, the traffic manager, and all the other specialists in the field.

Part of the problem arises out of the changing economic circumstances of the industry. When the railways enjoyed their virtual monopoly of inland transport, management was largely technical, and commercial judgement was relatively unimportant (it remained undervalued for many years after the monopoly was broken). Shipping faced the need to relate itself to land transport in an entirely new way as the movement of freight was transferred to the international container. The problems of traffic in towns make the provision of urban passenger transport the concern of the planners and economists in a way that the municipal transport manager of the 1930s could hardly have foreseen. And so the field of transport studies cannot be a closed one, but must accept the contributions of all the related disciplines while remaining true to the nature of the transport industry itself.

Even so, transport studies are not yet defined to everyone's agreement. There are those who would deny the very existence of a unified field, and the matter is still subject to debate in the academic world. Even the Institute of Logistics and Transport, the professional body for the industry, does not seem to have achieved the repute of the engineering institutions, for reasons which we shall examine in the next chapter.

In the academic world, transport studies departments are only now emerging from the tutelage of the older disciplines, notably civil engineering. The lack of a unified body of theory seems to be related to the discrete 'models' of transport that the academic disciplines have developed, each of which is inevitably weak when considered in isolation. Yet some progress does seem to have been made.

The original model was, not surprisingly, an engineering one, arising from the technological dominance of rail-born transport in the Railway Age. Its strength has been extended by the importance of road construction in more recent years, and its assumptions are basically those of the producer who can afford to wait for the consumer to come to him. During the past 40 years the growing crisis of public transport and increasing concern of governments with issues of transport policy have led to the development of an economic model which has had relatively little interaction with the pattern of technological constraints and opportunities. This model, while taking account of consumer demand, has found it difficult to allow for seemingly irrational behaviour on the part of human beings unwilling to act as expected by the notion of 'economic man'. Thus a third model, founded in the behavioural sciences, is necessary to complement the other two, and this is now slowly beginning to emerge.

As time goes on we may hope to see the integration of all three of these models, thus producing a unified theory of transport. Those commencing the study today may expect to see many changes, and will be able to take part in some of the most important developments in thought and practice that the twentieth century will have seen.

FOOTNOTE

[1] See his essay 'Do you remember Albuhera?', in Graves, *The Crane Bag*, Cassell, London, 1969.

3

The Function of Transport

Narrow and long the motor-bus
Lumbers round bend on bend

Charles Williams, *In a Motor-bus*

THE TRANSPORT PRODUCT

Transportants never seem quite to agree on whether they are engaged in an industry or in the provision of a professional service. At one extreme there is the railway with its long tradition of professionalism that leans heavily upon engineering; at the other there is haulage, where the small trader still plays a significant part. Shipping companies and airlines live in a world where their competitors are frequently state-subsidised, and where broader objectives have been widely held to override financial stability. People call for lower fares and, at the same time, for improved public transport, without recognising that subsidy means increased taxation as well as taking away the incentive for managers to innovate. Public debate as to the problems of transport might well be clarified if some agreement were to be reached on these issues.

All the same, whether transport is seen as an industry or a profession, it must have a product. We must now define this with some care as a basis for further discussion. If we leave aside loose definitions such as 'the provision of a service', and ask why people are prepared to pay for transport, it becomes clear that it depends upon what the economist calls 'derived demand'. Some people do enjoy travelling for its own sake, but for the majority of those who use passenger or freight services (including car-owners) transport is a means of getting themselves or their goods to some other place. It is this that makes speed of such extreme significance; for most people, time spent in transit is wasted time. Air freight services attract custom partly because their speed can reduce the non-productive time that goods spend in their forwarding. On the other hand, fares of about half those charged by the railways accounted in part for the growth of the slower express coach services before the motorway age.

The ultimate and unattainable objective of the development of transport is instantaneous movement from one place to another, at no cost. This gives a hint as to how we can define 'the product'. It is arrival that matters; everything else is related to the price and quality of the service, as to which we all have our own range of preferences. The only vital qualities are related to our wish to plan our own lives, and they may be summed up in a general definition:

The product of transport is safe arrival (whether of passengers or goods) in accordance with the advertised schedule.

Within this definition we allow the consumer's proper choice of mode, and above all we allow him to decide whether he prefers to economise and accept slower, less comfortable or less reliable transport at lower cost, or whether he is willing to pay more for better quality.

Now, a profession holds out the offer of a standard quality of service, whether or not it exists in practice. No doctor or lawyer offers cut prices yet, even though we all know that some are better at their job than others. And further, attempts to standardise transport charges have invariably ended in financial imbalance, and to a loss of quality to the consumer whose freedom of choice they ignored. Such an attempt was made with rail fares up until 1962, contributing no little to the decline of the railways. There is, on the other hand, a limit to the extent of choice that can be made available to the consumer, who can never expect to find the exact quality that suits his needs at a price that he is willing to pay.

So we may conclude that transport is an industry nicely balanced between business and professionalism. The great professional institutions, as in engineering in all its branches, exist because the public rightly requires assurance of the highest standards both of probity and expertise in such fields, even at the cost of higher charges than a more competitive dispensation might permit. In the provision of transport the factors of cheapness and of choice are of greater weight. The product is ephemeral, as distinct from that, say, of the bridge-building engineer; it perishes in the moment of production. Therefore we prefer to entrust the assurance of safety to the supervision of the state, and to retain a much greater element of competition in the provision of our transport services.

AIR TRANSPORT

The great and obvious divisions of the industry are those between land, sea and air transport, but when we speak of different modes of transport we mean something more complex than that. Air transport is a mode of itself, although the future may bring about a further subdivision through the development of rocket propulsion. Most people probably think of the airlines as passenger carriers, but air freight is growing extremely fast. The provision of airports and navigational aids are themselves subsidiary activities essential to commercial flying, and they function as a separate branch of the industry. The hovercraft is a hybrid, and we may debate whether to call it a vehicle or a vessel.

For freight, the special value of air transport is its speed, while the limited amount of space available in aircraft has encouraged the industry to concentrate largely upon the carriage of relatively small items. The fact that speed is important to the shipper in direct proportion to the value of the goods has led to the use of air freight services primarily for goods of high value, or extreme perishability. In recent years however, the competitive efficiency of air transport has attracted a wider range of commodities, including even railway locomotives.

For passengers, the aeroplane comes into its own when distances are above a certain limit, or when there are sea crossings to be avoided. The attraction of the hovercraft may be due to its combining the security of the ship with the stability and speed of the aircraft.

For inland transport, the speed advantage of the aeroplane is offset by the time it takes to travel to and from the airport, so that for distances up to at least 200 miles air is at a disadvantage compared with rail. Many of today's Train Operating Companies (TOCs) inherited from British Rail a pattern of high-speed services linking the principal British cities with each other and with London. Their success has stimulated low-cost air services over the longer distances, with some quite intense price competition. And with airports such as the three in London, and those at Manchester and Newcastle upon Tyne, having frequent, high-speed rail feeder services, the distance by which air travel has the advantage is by no means clear.

In the United States, where flying is much more readily accepted, the railway companies generally failed to use their advantage over medium distances, and largely opted out of passenger business. One consequence of this was that the federal government had to use public funds to re-establish passenger railway services.

RAIL TRANSPORT

Land transport may be divided into two modes, road and rail, although in practice there are subdivisions of these. The road transport industry is complex because, apart from the distinction between passenger and freight movement, there is also the division between public and private transport, both for passengers and goods. Then there is the difference between the provision of the 'infrastructure' and the actual movement of people and goods.

The advantage of rail passenger transport in competition with the airlines is clear, but while for longer distances the aeroplane does have the attraction of greater speed, experience shows that many people prefer to remain on the surface. This makes it likely that the railway will continue to connect all the main provincial cities with London, even though it may be at a disadvantage in comparison with air transport at the distances of Edinburgh and Glasgow.

What is clear for the immediate future is the healthy demand for fast, frequent and comfortable train services over such routes as London to Bristol, Birmingham, Manchester and Leeds. In concentrating upon this traffic, following the strategy outlined by Lord Beeching, British Rail was often criticised for neglecting branch lines and intermediate small towns. But the logic of the policy is supported by its success. The Beeching Report[1] defined the place of the railway as a long-haul bulk carrier, whether of passengers or goods; the equivalent of the motor lorry, the coach or the car being the whole train, not the individual rail vehicle.

In the passenger business this means persuading as many people as possible to ride together as far as possible. In large cities, the numbers of people who can be carried on one train may be sufficient to outweigh the short distance over which they wish to travel, and then the urban railway (usually underground) becomes justified. But urban transport has its own special problems, associated with subjects like land-use planning and with urban government in general, so that it is really a special field on its own.

THE URBAN PROBLEM

The answers to urban problems are not easily found. There are those who advocate the draconian measure of banning the private car from city centres, but a little thought will show how impracticable this would be. A wide range of exceptions would have to be permitted if justice were to be done, so that a new bureaucracy would be required to administer the system, while the legislation would create so many hard cases that the effect in public ill-will might be insurmountable. When we add the very real advantages of the private car that would be denied to so many people, including the disabled, we have to accept that the policy would impoverish urban residents in an arbitrary fashion; a cost to be set against any benefits that might be obtained. Those who support such measures ought in fairness to declare whether or not they themselves habitually drive cars in cities.

The possibility of road-pricing as an alternative becomes immediately attractive, however difficult we find it to swallow the idea of paying for the use of the highway. But road-pricing may be seen as another form of taxation, and motorists may well feel they are paying enough already. We have to accept the fact that the private car is now an effective part of the transport system, owned by people at all levels of society, and not just a rather undesirable alternative to public transport available only to the rich. Its place has yet to be defined in an acceptable way, but perhaps road-pricing, which leaves a real choice to the car-owner, can help us to define it.

While the supremacy of the bus for urban public transport is unlikely to be disturbed, recent years have seen the 'return of the rail' in the form of Light Rapid Transit (LRT). This is neither a new kind of train nor a return to the old kind of tram, but it is to be found in a number of different guises. On Tyneside and in Greater Manchester the rail cars use former suburban railways, with tunnels in the centre of Newcastle and street running in Manchester; a similar system is to be found in Croydon. The controversial Sheffield 'Supertram' is almost all street-running, while the West Midlands Line One depends upon a long-disused railway track, with street running in Birmingham and Wolverhampton. In London, the Docklands Light Railway is a system quite unlike any of the others, while Liverpool is planning to re-introduce the trolleybus.

An alternative system, still more of a hybrid, is the Kerb-Guided Bus (KGB), where standard road vehicles run on special sections of track, guided by a wheel-bearing on the raised kerb. Sections of KGB can be used to give the buses priority on busy roads, and the system has the advantage of allowing bus routes to 'fan out' to serve the suburbs, avoiding the necessity for passengers to change. KGB is also very much cheaper to construct and maintain, and it may well limit the development of LRT, and of new 'heavy railways', to locations where special circumstances apply.

Rail freight

It used to seem obvious that the most important function of rail transport was the carriage of freight. This may have had something to do with the North American experience, where distances are so much greater. Trains well over a mile long, with up to five locomotives spaced out along them, carry heavy loads at competitive charges. Yet we have already seen that the US railways failed to keep a serious hold on the passenger business. Conditions in this country are different. We have seen the transfer of the great bulk of the nation's freight from rail to road transport over the past 25 years. At the same time, the changing pattern of British industry, in which the heavy industries are now so much less important, together with the shrinking demand for coal, has meant that much of the traditional railway freight traffic no longer moves at all.

The railways' answer to this challenge was the freightliner With more and more of the goods available for carriage being in the category of 'merchandise', rather than in bulk, the railways were faced with the problem of how to make up large enough loads to suit their own characteristics. Their answer was to encourage the trader to load his own container, to be carried over the greater part of its journey by fast train, with no need to load and unload the cargo at each end of the rail journey. The scheme has the further potential that it can pay freight forwarders to collect consignments from a wide area and make up similar unit loads for the railway to carry, which they may be better able to do than the railways themselves. Thus the freightliner is in part a chance for the railways to take advantage of their competitor's strength.

In the later years of British Rail the movement of goods by train declined, but since privatisation, and with government grants for terminal facilities, there has been a significant increase. Length of haul is important, and the Channel Tunnel has opened up new possibilities, with dedicated terminals at various places in the North and the Midlands. But sometimes a regular series of train-load consignments over a short distance, so that the locomotives and wagons are almost constantly moving, can be as economic as freight moving over much longer distances.

Motive power

The question of motive power for railways has been debated for many years, and policy in Britain is to electrify the system. Diesel traction, however, originally seen as an interim stage between steam and electricity, proved more efficient than expected, as well as being less expensive to install. It is still broadly true that only the busiest lines can justify the cost of building an electric system, while the supposed appeal of electric traction to the passenger has certainly been overrated.

Speed and comfort attract traffic. The fact that electrification usually implies new and improved carriages to ride in is merely adventitious. All this was abundantly proved by the success of British Rail's Inter City 125 trains in attracting custom by high standards of quality. Nevertheless, energy prospects and environmental protection may well influence investment policy towards more widespread electrification in the future.

ROAD TRANSPORT

It is a commonplace that the railways have suffered from the development of the internal combustion engine; it is as well to remember that this did not at first mean the private car.

One of the most revolutionary changes in the transport of passengers, comparable almost to the introduction of the steam railway, has been the growth of car ownership since 1950. The impact of this has been felt equally by the railways and the buses. In comparison, the impact of private motoring upon the railways in earlier years was negligible; it was the motor bus and coach (even more than the lorry) that ended the Railway Age.

The impact of road haulage upon railway traffic has thus been at its greatest in the past 50 years. Originally limited by size and mechanical efficiency, the motor lorry at first catered mainly for local traffic, and was slowly adopted by the railways themselves for collection and delivery purposes. By 1938 the haulage industry was covering the longer distances, but it was the post-war years that saw the improvement of the vehicle to the position of an effective alternative to rail-carried freight.

The truck has the enormous advantage of being able to reach the customer's premises without having to transfer the load. Unless the consignment is large enough for the freightliner, or the customer has a private siding, the railway has no way of equalling this. The short-haul use of the road vehicle is also still of the greatest importance. Statistically it is likely that the heavy lorry holding up the motorist's passage across a city is making a journey for which the railway is quite unsuited. But the most remarkable impact of motor transport has probably been in the field of distribution.

Just over a half of the goods carried by heavy goods vehicles in 1997 went in lorries or vans used mainly for 'own-account' transport, that is to say vehicles used for the goods of those who own them, and not the fleets of the public carriers. The advent of motor transport has also done much to promote the growth of 'national' products, available in every shop or public house in the kingdom. Modern marketing is dependent upon road transport far more than upon rail.

Business logistics

The link between marketing and transport has come to sponsor a new development: the branch of the industry that came under the head of physical distribution management has expanded into a new field of study, called business logistics. Here the function of transport in all its modes as a means of distributing goods is integrated with the broader concept of distribution; with warehousing; with the mathematics of route planning and costing; with packaging and stock control; with the siting and layout of customer outlets; and – over all these – with the notion of inventory costs, which effective logistics must reduce to a minimum. (Inventory costs include the interest on capital tied up in the system and in goods-in-transit; time costs like insurance; and avoidable costs like overheads on premises, vehicles, etc) With the spread of 'Just-in-time' (JIT) management in much of industry, which means that raw materials or components are delivered as required, with no stocks being held, business logistics now applies to manufacture well as distribution of goods.

Regulation and deregulation

Road haulage legislation

The road haulage industry expanded from being a largely short-haul and feeder activity in the 1920s to become a threat to the railways in the following decade. Nevertheless it has always been marked by a prevalence of small firms, some of which subcontract work from the larger ones. A licensing system introduced in 1933 to protect the railway companies was dismantled in 1968, when it was found to have functioned at the cost of greater efficiency. Today the purpose of legislation is to ensure high quality in the construction and use of the vehicles, which we shall examine later on.

Bus and coach legislation and development

Bus and coach services developed in overt competition with the railways, and in the 1920s they took a good deal of trade from the train services. On balance, it seems likely that the buses brought as much traffic to the railways as they took away, but the long distance coaches, which spread rapidly after their introduction in 1925, were an immediate threat to railway finances. Bus services today fulfil a number of separate functions, linked by the flexibility of the vehicle, which does not necessarily require to be specially designed or adapted for each of them.

First among these functions is the provision of long-distance services. The network of express coach routes now forms an essential part of the transport system, partly because of the closure of many railways, but also because of a substantial preference for coach travel. It would be quite wrong to regard the coaches as a second-class system, for in fact there is a complete network of routes covering the country throughout the year, used by people of every social class, even if mainly from the older and younger age groups. To the extent that the coaches, not being allowed to carry standing passengers, offer a guaranteed seat, they have an advantage over the railways, quite apart from their lower fares.

At one time the motor coach (to use an old-fashioned term) had to compete with the trains on cost alone, since it was not really in the same bracket in either speed or comfort. Many people in any case preferred the train because of the chance to move about on a long trip, and the availability of toilet and refreshment facilities. But there has been a quite remarkable change since the first edition of this book appeared in 1970.

The availability of motorways played a part in this, although they were widely used before the expansion of coach traffic began. The two factors that changed the competitive situation were, first, the Transport Act of 1980, which freed long distance coach services from quantity and price control, and second the arrival at roughly the same time of a new generation of 'super-coaches', whose design had been pioneered on the Continent.

Marketed as 'Rapide', the new services offered individual reclining seats, on-board toilets, and steward or stewardess service of light refreshments; even telephones appeared on some of the vehicles. Although they remain slower than trains over comparable journeys, the difference is markedly less, while the overall quality of the very top level coach services must compare favourably with standard class by train.

Perhaps for most people the bus is identified with the next function, a provider of urban services. London, Glasgow,

Liverpool and Newcastle upon Tyne are the only British cities with a purely urban railway, and few others rely substantially upon suburban railways. The traditional electric tramway is no more, while the trolley-bus may seem a slightly improbable compromise of a temporary nature. In its day, the tramcar was regarded as a proletarian vehicle, while the motor bus, serving the less densely populated parts of our towns, had a middle-class air. Later on, the distinction was lost and the bus came to be associated with the 'less well-to-do'.

The process was partly the result of increased car ownership, although the car quickly ceased to be solely a middle-class possession. It was also associated with the need for public transport to have a substantial concentration of demand to be financially viable. The greater the investment, the greater the need for high levels of use, such as are still concentrated mainly in working-class districts and rehousing schemes. But at the same time there was a tendency in most British cities, most marked in the 1970s, for public transport operators to seek greater labour productivity by running large conductorless double-deck buses, which necessitated lower frequencies to carry an equivalent volume of traffic. By the end of the decade, urban bus transport had become more and more unattractive, and was requiring an increasing amount of state subsidy.

The 1980s saw a series of changes that would have seemed impossible in 1980. The minibus, which had been dismissed as a possible solution to the urban transport problem (despite its use in many cities, such as Buenos Aires, where European conditions of traffic apply), was introduced in 1984 with immediate success in the city of Exeter. In 1986 the effect of deregulation and of the ending of indiscriminate subsidy to bus operators produced a variety of new approaches to the problem, including the return of conductors in some cities, and the use of minibuses, either alone or in association with trad-itional double-deckers, in many more. The down-market image of public transport may be starting to reverse.

Experience in the United States has shown that it is not a wise social policy so to reconstruct a city that it can be dependent solely on the private car. In any event, the cost in both money and in lost amenity is such that few people in

Britain would be likely to want it. But we have seen that the alternative of a city in which the private car is banned is not only impossible to impose (if people are to be allowed cars to get out of the city, how can they be prevented from using them within it?); it is also a policy of impoverishment. Yet at present the car and the bus, within the fiscal system of this country, are deadly enemies, combining to create a state of affairs in which neither can function efficiently.

Faced with the manifest inability of the bus industry to resolve the problem in the 1970s, a general consensus developed among the political parties that something should be done about the structure of control within which the industry worked. In 1979 the Liberal manifesto was the only one to promise the removal of licensing restrictions, but in 1980 the Conservative government made the first step in this direction, by doing away with the control of bus fares. One effect of this was the development of area-wide travelcards in many places; another was the encouragement of young and enthusiastic managers to develop creative pricing policies that would encourage the use of buses (as railway management had done after being freed from price control in 1962). For the 1983 election, both Labour and the Liberals took fright, and promised closer control over the industry, while the Conservatives spoke of privatisation.

In the event, the government accepted the recommendations of a number of leading economists, and published in 1984 a White Paper simply called *Buses*, in which it outlined a programme of deregulation and privatisation (though it baulked at road-use pricing), that was enacted in 1985 and put into effect on 26 October 1986. The opposition parties and trade unions, with orthodox opinion in the industry, united to oppose the programme, which also included an outright ban on indiscriminate subsidy and was introduced at the same time as the spending powers of local authorities were severely restricted by 'rate-capping'. The predicted disasters did not befall, although there were severe problems in some of the former metropolitan counties where management had been given too short a time to prepare for the combined effect of competition, restructuring and the new arrangements for subsidy. The state-owned companies had been able to plan for competition but faced restructuring later.

Now that the dust has settled, and many of the older generation of bus managers who disapproved of the new policies have taken early retirement, the reforms of 1980 and 1985 are generally accepted as having benefited the industry, and a return to the old regime seems most improbable. It may yet take some time before firm conclusions can be reached, but it is fair to say that the consumer now attracts far more attention than used to be the case. It is no mean achievement that today 61 per cent of households in the eight largest conurbations have a bus nearby every 15 minutes.

Outside the cities there are inter-urban and rural bus services. These are best discussed together because the boundary between them is not always easy to define. Where population is thinly spread, the importance of the private car is proportionately greater, for no bus network could be expected to bring public transport to every door, or even within miles of it. For this reason the density of cars tends to vary inversely with the density of people, yet even here, 52 per cent of households have at least one bus every hour.

While country people may also be more self-sufficient, requiring to make fewer journeys for their needs, there are still many people who do not have the use of a car when they need it. In catering for these people, the bus does not serve the same function as it does in the town; a bus once a week to the local market centre may well be an 'adequate' service. Seaside excursions in the summer may supplement the schedule, and shopping trips once a year to the big city. Here it must be remembered that the public services may not be the half of the tale; clubs and societies have their outings, and not least of these are run by the Women's Institutes. There are even buses run under contract to take people to play bingo.

The old problem of maintaining services that are not commercially justified was tackled under the Transport Act of 1985 by giving the counties and metropolitan districts the responsibility for identifying such needs, and inviting tenders from operators for providing a facility. (This applies equally where off-peak and other non-commercial urban services are concerned.) As a result, the councils in some places have almost become bus operators in their own right, requiring successful tenderers to adopt the council's corporate image.

But much of the countryside today is coming within the orbit of the towns, as people settle farther and farther out and either commute to work or take jobs that involve travelling widely by car. For these areas the problem is how best to provide a stand-by service for occasions when the car is not available, and how to cater for people who cannot make use of the car. The function of the bus is changing in this field as well, and it is not yet clear how it will adapt itself, but the flexibility of the industry is such that a solution will sooner or later be found.

The network of inter-urban services has of course replaced the railway for short-distance purposes, and these services are also part of the rural provision where they serve villages and hamlets along their route. Here too the private car offers serious competition, especially because it is so much quicker; the motor bus still 'lumbers round bend on bend', as did the one Charles Williams rode in . . .

> Leaning against the end
> For a long hour . . .
> . . . (as) once from Golder's Green we went
> Down into Hertfordshire . . .[2]

In the past it was the smaller firms that tended to run coaches with heating and doors, before the larger ones that run most of the services realised the need for luxuries like those. Now the next step forward must be the use of faster, lighter buses that can begin to compare with the private car in terms of speed.

Another function of the bus, largely found outside the towns, is the carriage of school children and work people on services run under contract. The former traffic originated quite early, with the drive to offer grammar school places to children from all parts of the country. Since 1945 it has been greatly increased as the bus has been used to enable small primary schools to be closed, with consequent savings to the education service. This has been a very important aspect of the social impact of the bus on the rural community. It has had its unfortunate side, with the disappearance of the village school from so many small parishes, but the contract buses, on the other hand, made it possible for many people to continue to live in the countryside who would otherwise have been driven to the towns by the rapid shrinkage in the agricultural labour force.

It will be seen now that the function of the bus and coach industry is by no means limited to the provision of scheduled services, and the last example to be considered is its use for excursions and tours, either advertised or privately arranged. The importance of this sort of service in country areas has already been described, and something similar applies in most built-up areas as well. Because of the diffuse layout of our cities, rail services from the centre involve the passenger in lengthy journeys before joining a train. For all sorts of purposes, the coach running from the suburbs has a great attraction. A specialised example of this is the extended tour, whether running within Britain or overseas, which commenced early in the history of the industry and still continues to attract demand.

MARINE TRANSPORT

Railways and road transport are essentially concerned with internal movements, yet both have an interest in traffic going overseas. In the movement of freight, this is of increasing importance with the development of container traffic, and the roll-on-roll-off ferry that enables road vehicles to be used as if the seas no longer divided Britain from Ireland or the European continent. The overland routes to India via Iran and to West Africa via the Mediterranean ferries and the Sahara were proved to be viable, while the Trans-Siberian Railway offered a 'land bridge' to China and Japan. The British network of public long-distance coach services has been slow to develop in Europe, but shuttle services to the Spanish resorts enjoyed a boom until airlines succeeded in offering lower prices to the tour organisers.

Ferry services across the narrow seas to Europe have become big business, both for freight transport and for the holiday-makers travelling in the family car. The 'classic passenger', travelling by train and ship, has ceased to be the principal customer of the 'packet boats', and the ferries themselves have become mini-liners, with every kind of entertainment on board. So rapid has their growth been that safety regulations have not always been kept up with ship design and management, with tragic results that are well known. Formerly an extension of the railways into another mode, they are now owned by a number of highly competitive holding companies.

The ferries are in competition with the airlines, and many of them compete with the Channel Tunnel, itself a form of ferry, carrying cars and commercial vehicles as well as providing a train service. For journeys by each mode between two countries in the European Union the withdrawal of duty-free regulations must have an effect on prices, but this seems likely to affect the shipping companies more severely than the airlines or the Tunnel.

Apart from the ferries, the narrow seas are the province of a multitude of small to medium-sized ships engaged in freight transport, as well as larger ones that use the bigger ports. Timber from northern Europe arrives in vessels little more than coasters, loaded to the gunwale with deck cargo and crossing the North Sea in all weathers to call at small ports like Wisbech or Scarborough as well as bigger ones like Grimsby and the Tees. General cargo is carried from places such as Great Yarmouth and Whitstable, while from the smaller ports on the south coast there are ships that carry mixed cargoes to France and return with wine from the Loire. Amongst them all are the tankers, which make up the bulk of the remaining coastal trade, carrying petrol and chemicals from the refineries to the smaller ports, or transhipping oil from the supertankers that unload at sea, in such places as Lyme Bay, since when fully loaded they draw too much to enter port.

Much freight across the narrow seas, as we have already seen, moves by the container ships and roll-on-roll-off ferries. Whether they come to the port by road or rail, the vehicles and containers form the 'cargo', and their contents make no difference. The principle behind this traffic is the same that we have already discussed in connection with the deep sea container ships, and its economies are changing the pattern of shipping in the narrow seas as much as upon the open oceans of the world.

The new techniques are turning the ships of the narrow seas into a series of ferries, and in a sense this is true of ocean shipping too. The aeroplane has taken so much of the passenger traffic that the old concept of the passenger liner is now out of date. Cruising has become more and more popular, and the idea of a voyage as holiday is being sold as a package. Once the 'Queens' and their competitors were the Atlantic ferry, while today their successors are the leisurely complement to the aircraft that provide the basic service for passengers.

At the same time the growth of containerisation is making the freight liner much more of a ferry in the deep sea trades as well. But here we find signs of another change, which is just beginning. The world's trade routes are themselves the product of history, and in particular of the dominance of Western Europe. By clinging too long to sail, the Yankee shipowners lost their significance as the nineteenth century saw the steamship emerge. The growth of the colonial empires of Britain, France, Holland and Germany settled shipping lines (and subsequently airlines) into a pattern still recognisable today. It was a pattern that assumed the concentration of primary industries in a few countries of the western world which supplied others with their products in return for food and certain raw materials. The self-sufficiency of the United States and Russia kept them largely out of this pattern, but the developing countries are now beginning to ask whether it is a pattern that can serve their needs in the future.

But the organisation of shipping depends not only upon the trade routes of the world. The commodities of world trade, combined with the development of the technical potential of the ship, have increasingly made for specialisation, and the history of shipping is one in which the all-purpose vessel has been steadily superseded. The irony of containerisation is the sense in which this process has been set upon its head in the carriage of general merchandise.

The familiar division of merchant ships into types lay between 'tramps' and liners, with tankers appearing as a third variety as the twentieth century wore on. Generally the tramp dealt with bulk freights as and where they were to be found, while the liner carried general merchandise, with or without passengers, and offered speed and regularity of advertised sailing to offset the higher charges that such trading must imply. The distinction was never hard and fast – liner firms would charter tramp ships when cargoes were easy to come by – but it meant something even to the layman.

The changes we are seeing today have not yet run their course, but it is clear that the liner as we have known her is an anachronism. For a time she could double with cruising to make a living, but for freight she soon became uneconomic in comparison with the container ship, which can carry out so many more voyages in a lifetime. The bulk carrier is replacing the tramp, but then the bulk carrier is really a tramp doing a regular run with the same commodity between the same ports. Being far larger, she cannot economically enter a trade where the ship must go to the cargo wherever it is to be found. (She is also extremely efficient, and has revolutionised the location of the steel industry both in Britain and throughout the world.) The tanker is now seen to be a special sort of bulk carrier.

But the shipping industry has changed more than once in its history, and while it has the special problem that its vessels cost so much more to construct than the vehicles of any other branch of transport, it will without doubt adapt itself to the new world that is requiring such a change. Just what shape the new institutions of shipping will take it may still be too early to say.

FOOTNOTES

[1] The Reshaping of British Railways, HMSO, London, 1963.
[2] Charles Williams, 'In a Motor-bus', included in *Divorce*, Oxford University Press, Oxford, 1920.

4

The Control of Transport

'Home Rails' have vanished; 'Transport Stock' is here

Gilbert Thomas, *Nostalgia*

BACKGROUND

Transport has never been considered an industry quite like others. In the Middle Ages, when the Justices settled 'the just price', they had control over carriers' charges as well as over bread. The post was from early days a royal prerogative, and this came to mean the provision of horses for 'travelling post' as well as the carriage of the mail. The idea that travel is something of a luxury, suitable, like smoking, for a sumptuary tax, was expressed in the substantial tax burden carried by the stagecoaches. There was also nominally a mileage duty of one halfpenny a mile on every four passengers levied on the railways (they were allowed to compound for a much lower sum) until the end of the nineteenth century. It is the same idea that appears to govern the taxation of the motor car today. The taxation of food has been repulsive to the British since the

44

repeal of the Corn Laws in 1846, but the taxation of travel has not always been seen in quite the same light.

Shipping

Shipping was for many years an industry considered so vital to the welfare of the nation that it was given statutory protection under the Navigation Acts. And when the reforming government of 1849 proposed their repeal it was widely held that such a measure would be disastrous. Yet it has been said that to their repeal we owe 'more than to any single factor' the subsequent healthy development of the British merchant marine.[1] By a stroke of irony the same government, faced with the 'lack of professional standards in the shipping industry', was forced to pass an 'Act for improving the condition of Masters, Mates and Seamen and maintaining discipline in the Merchant Service'; an Act upon whose foundation has been built a complex structure of control that governs every aspect of the life of a ship and her crew.

   With the mechanisation of transport the need for the state to intervene became inescapable, while the practice of such intervention tended to change. Now safety became the over-riding concern of parliament; safety of the passenger, and to some extent of the crew, and safety of the 'third party' – the individual, not being a traveller, who might, for example, be run down by a train in the legitimate course of his business. For shipping the interest ended there, for the principles of free trade required the shipowner to be left alone to conduct his bargaining and make what profit he might, but the special nature of rail transport introduced a further element of control. This is the element of price control, which, while it has been applied from time to time in the case of air, rail and bus services, has never been attempted for either shipping or road haulage in this country. What we come up against here is the extent to which any mode of transport may be seen to benefit from some degree of monopoly that would justify regulation of its prices so as to prevent the customer from exploitation. Competition, on the other hand, can be relied upon to hold prices down.

Railways

The medieval system of regulating carriers' rates had disappeared by the time the stagecoaches appeared, but with the development of canals and turnpike roads, both of which required parliamentary sanction, the state was forced to take a new interest. It was realised that each of these new modes of transport would consist of a series of monopolies, and that it would therefore be necessary to protect passengers and traders from exploitation. This was normally done by settling maximum tolls.

But although the turnpike trusts and the canal companies were large concerns for their day, it was the development of the railway system that forced parliament over a long period to accept the wider responsibilities for control which have affected transport policy ever since. Like the canals and turnpikes, the railways could not be built without parliamentary sanction. They needed this in order to obtain the powers of compulsory purchase without which railway promoters could have been held to ransom by landowners (even so, high prices for land affected the course of many lines). Even more, they needed it to obtain the privilege of limited liability, without which they could not have raised the capital they required. No general company legislation had been introduced, and each railway company was therefore the product of an individual Act.

That the laissez-faire administrations of the nineteenth century were thus obliged to accept the railways as a special case, and to erect a body of state control over them, is less ironical than it might at first sight appear. The theory of economics propounded by Adam Smith and developed by Cobden, Bright and Ricardo never contemplated a monopoly left unchecked by the state, and the control of railways was sanctioned by the strictest canons of laissez-faire. The fact that such control was slow in being applied is accounted for by the unwillingness of parliament to accept the monopolistic nature of railways, which gave rise to a long period of ambivalent and often contradictory policy.[2]

The essentially British invention of the modern railway was exported the world over. With the exception of the Americas, where laissez-faire was a similar guiding principle, railways tended to be built with more or less state planning (in Prussia for military purposes, in Belgium to unite the newly founded state). There is some evidence that laissez-faire produced a network similar to anything evolved by state planning, and that it did so with less delay.

But from their earliest days there were those in Britain who argued that the railways should be owned and even operated by the state, and Gladstone's Act of 1844 provided powers for the nationalisation of railways authorised after its passage, at the expiry of 21 years. No use was ever made of these powers, but it is well to remember that the idea of public ownership of railways has a long and respectable history. For the most part, though, nineteenth-century parliaments were concerned lest the monopolistic nature of a railway should be used by the companies to the disadvantage of trade, and to the danger of the public. The surveillance of railways was made the respons- ibility of the Board of Trade, and a body of regulation grew up which was comparable with that established for shipping.

But while the shipping industry was regulated solely in terms of technical standards and the safety and welfare of passengers and crew, the railway regulations went further and interfered with the commercial freedom of the companies. From 1854 onwards the price control which had been applied to individual railways from the first, in the form of maximum rates, was reinforced by both general and specific legislation. This took the form of an overall prohibition of 'undue prefer- ence' (discrimination between customers), supported by the requirement that the companies should publish their freight rates, and by the gradual establishment of scales of charging. By the beginning of the First World War, the conclusion had been reached that railway competition was largely meaning- less, and that it was logical to extend control still further. As a consequence, the 121 companies still existing in 1921 were required to group themselves into four,[3] and a new charging policy was devised which, while it simplified the rate structure, was expected to produce an annual revenue thought reasonable for reinvestment and the remuneration of shareholders.

The Railways Act of 1921 suffered from the fundamental weakness that is assumed the continuance of the railways' shared monopoly. The grouping came into effect in 1923, and implied of course a management reorganisation of the most extensive kind (except in the case of the GWR, the one company that remained from pre-grouping days). The new scale of charging became effective only in 1928. In the meantime there had been the General Strike of 1926, which had shown that the railways were no longer the indispensable national asset they had previously been considered to be. In its essence, the strike was an attempt to paralyse the life of the nation as much by the withdrawal of transport services as by anything else (much of manufacturing industry was unaffected). But the motor transport industry, hardly organised outside of London by any union, proved itself capable of replacing the railways, at least for emergency purposes, and thus contributed largely to the collapse of the strike.

Motorised transport

The motor transport industry had grown up largely free from public control (the main exception being the provision of urban transport in many towns and cities). By the end of the 1920s the railways – tied as they were by statutory regulation – had been severely affected by the preference of traders and passengers for road services, generally at lower prices. A Royal Commission recommended the introduction of a licensing scheme for road transport that would achieve, in their words, 'rationalisation as a prelude to nationalisation'.[4] The nationalisation of all forms of transport and communications had in fact been the aim of Lloyd George and Sir Eric Geddes at the end of the First World War, and when the Ministry of Transport was set up in 1919, with Geddes as the first minister, a skeleton organisation was established to take the railways over.

During the 1930s licensing systems were introduced – for road passenger services in 1930 and for freight in 1933. In the meantime the railways had in 1929 obtained formal powers to run road services themselves, which they used in order to buy an interest in the newer industry. The licensing system for buses and coaches followed the precedent of parliamentary control of railway charging by limiting the commercial freedom of the operators, while it also and quite separately achieved a great improvement in the technical standards of the industry.

Air transport

The expansion of road transport into a fully viable industry took place during the remarkably short period from 1919 to 1929, but of course it was based upon pre-war pioneer operations. The air transport industry on the other hand, cannot be said to have effectively begun operations until after the First World War, and its development for the following two decades was uncertain and erratic. The state seemed unable to decide whether commercial flying should be subsidised or not, and while at first the need for subsidy was inescapable, during the early 1930s a few independent firms (one or two of them launched by bus operators) were showing how effective they could be. The 'chosen instrument' of government policy, Imperial Airways, on the other hand, was the subject of severe criticism in press and parliament. The four railway companies also entered air transport, largely on a joint basis with other operators, but the decade ended with the establishment in August 1939 of a nationalised corporation, the British Overseas Airways Corporation, which acquired Imperial and also British Airways. In 1946, the process was taken further by the acquisition of the railways' interests and of the remaining independents, and by the formation of British European Airways.

NATIONALISATION

With the return of a Labour administration in 1945, nationalisation of transport was widely considered to be inevitable, whether or not one approved of it in principle – and we must remember that state ownership of the railways had been advocated before the war by people of every political persuasion. As early as 1949, however, independent airlines were permitted to fly regular services as 'associates' of the nationalised corporations, while large parts of inland surface transport remained exempt from nationalisation. Railways, however, came into public ownership almost entirely, the exceptions being industrial sidings and works lines, and those provided by various associations and companies as 'living museums'.

The Transport Act of 1947 set up the British Transport Commission (BTC), which immediately acquired the four railway companies, the London Passenger Transport Board, the canals, and such of the docks as were in railway ownership, along with the railways' road transport in investments. The BTC was also given instructions to acquire the greater part of the 'long haul' road haulage industry, and to prepare schemes for the integration of rail and road passenger services, for which it would be expected to acquire a further holding in the bus and coach industry. The Act also provided that the various transport responsibilities of the Commission should be managed by executives, which in practice enjoyed considerable independence. The Railway Executive actually followed policies that were at odds with those of the Commission itself.[5]

To obtain the full value of common ownership, and thereby to achieve the co-ordination of transport that was generally held to be desirable, priority was given to a system of differential charges reflecting the characteristics of the various modes of internal transport.[6] No provision for this was built into the 1947 Act; it is this that now seems the principal weakness of the past-war legislation. In its early years, the BTC was naturally preoccupied with the business of acquisitions and with the reorganisation of its possessions, while from the early 1950s the increasing railway deficit attracted much of its attention. As a consequence the work of co-ordination in any meaningful sense was never undertaken.

THE CAR-OWNERSHIP BOOM

Thus the nationalisation of transport may be seen as something of a non-event since the opportunities that it offered for a coherent and rational policy imposed from above were hardly taken. In many ways, the grouping of the railway companies in 1923 seems now to have been more significant. But the post-war period was marked by a revolution in transport comparable with the early development of railways and steamships; the inland transport industry shifted, as it were, its centre of gravity.

In the movement of freight, traditionally the more profitable side of the railways' activity, road transport had come to carry 81 per cent of the nation's goods by 1986. On the passenger side, the railways' share of the traffic had dropped to 7 per cent by the same date. But here the buses and coaches had not benefited, for the share of the private car had risen to 82 per cent.[7]

The background to this change was largely a matter of choice. No-one who has owned a car can doubt the inherent advantages of having one's own means of transport. It is hard for those who proclaim themselves superior to the private car to avoid the accusation of 'sour grapes'. This is not to deny the counter-attraction of public transport, which enables one to relax and to work or converse, and which is in many cases quicker. On balance, though, the car has proved itself more attractive for a great many people on a great many journeys. It makes travel with small children much easier; it has made a whole range of new social activities possible over a greatly increased distance; and it has transformed the commercial traveller of yesterday's train into the trade representative of today's private car. Above all, the car has widened beyond measure the choice of employment.

But benefits of this kind must be measured in terms of money. The spread of car ownership had been made possible by its falling cost, at a time when public transport has grown more expensive in real terms. Here there have been several forces at work, the first being the steady cheapening of the true cost of new and second-hand cars. The testing of cars for safety removes the very cheap second-hand vehicles from the market, but it is remarkable that the price index for cars was three points lower in 1967 than it had been in 1953, and 20 points lower than it had been in 1957. Since 1980 it has consistently risen less than the overall price index, while the opposite has been true for bus and coach travel.

At the same time, the running cost of all forms of transport rose. While this was sharp in the case of public transport, the running cost of motor vehicles went up less than the cost of living over a similar period. Thus we have a situation where the more attractive form of transport has also been increasingly the cheaper one, and we must not wonder at the consequences of this change.

We should indeed be grateful, for travel has increased in volume, and travel contributes to the quality of living. Over the ten years to 1967, household expenditure on travel (that is, on the transport element, excluding payments for hotels and meals) rose an average of £3.27 to £10.90 per week; the greatest increase being in expenditure on the purchase and running of private cars.[8] The *percentage* expenditure on transport and travel remained almost unchanged, increased affluence accounting for the shift to the private car.

Behind these figures lies the hard fact that the cost of providing public transport rose consistently over 20 years and that a very substantial proportion of this increase was due to the rising cost of labour. Let it be said at once that this was largely justified: not only has transport tended to be noted for low pay (balanced of course by security of employment, now in turn lost) but it happens also to be an industry in which men and women have to work at times when others are at leisure. In addition, it must be remembered that an industry offering low pay will attract poor staff, and above all will fail to attract the young people whose ability is needed to maintain progress and development. These were the economic facts of life for public transport during the years of full employment. The total cost of private motoring has a far smaller content of wages.

THE TREND TOWARDS DEREGULATION

It is against this background that we have to see the steady growth of the railway deficit each year from 1953, and the actual operating losses incurred after 1956. The bus and coach industry, faced with similar problems, was able to contract as demand fell so that its financial problems were less serious. But for the first ten years of the railway deficit, the BTC continued to provide a level of service beyond anything justified by public need.

The Beeching Report

The Transport Act of 1962 and the new policies that derived from the appointment of Dr Richard Beeching (later Lord Beeching) to the management of the new Railways Board changed this. For the first time, the railways were able to charge whatever prices they chose for the sale of their services, and encouraged to pick and choose their traffics. Whatever its weaknesses, the Beeching Report represented a new philosophy of transport, and identified the strengths and weaknesses of the railway in a way that had never been done quite so clearly before. The policies that followed from that analysis were driven through, sometimes with great force, and the railways in a remarkably short time began to take shape as a fighting unit, concerned more with progress than with tradition. Deficits have a disastrous effect on the morale of a commercial undertaking, and this had been especially noticeable in British Railways; after the reversal of the trend, railwaymen were able to recover a pride in their industry.

It may be said that transport is not a 'commercial undertaking', and that it is perfectly possible to finance it entirely by payments out of general taxation, making no charge to the user. There are substantial arguments against this, not least the indiscriminate use of scarce economic resources and the difficulty of knowing whether or not people are getting what they really want in the consequent monopoly situation. But such a major change of policy does not seem practical today, for it would imply severe restraint on our freedom to use the private car. (The alternative, of bringing home to us the cost of motoring, by some form of road-use pricing, is only now being taken seriously.)

The British Transport Commission

Throughout most of the twentieth century there was an increasing tendency for the transport industry to come under closer control by the state, and even into outright public ownership. In 1947 parliament foresaw the eventual emergence of a public body – the British Transport Commission, set up by the Transport Act of that year – that should be responsible for the provision of public transport by land of all kinds; it had been the dream of Sir Eric Geddes in 1919. Quite probably, most people who thought about this policy saw the railways as central to the Commission's function, just as Sir Henry Maybury had seen railed transport as of central importance in the 1920s and 1930s. The fact that we have seen (in the previous chapter) how railways were to lose out to road transport must not blind us to the way things seemed then. But the dream of a single, integrated management for the whole inland transport industry, still favoured by some, proved impossible to realise, and the decentralisation of ownership and control has been the pattern of history ever since.

To begin with, the Commission was not given responsibility for the whole industry. 'Own-account' transport was not affected by nationalisation, due to the resistance of the Co-operative Societies to give up their own delivery fleets. Neither were Labour-controlled city councils much pleased when the Commission sought to take over their buses and trams. Further-more, the structure of the Commission and its executives was in effect unworkable; the Railway Executive actually pursued policies that were contradictory to those of the Commission, and deliberately misled its superior authority. In any case; the Commission quickly became pre-occupied with the pressing problems of the railways, as the deficit grew during the 1950s, so that the other executives – London Transport, Docks and

Inland Waterways, Road Transport and so on – were left to their own devices. And, so far as the railways were concerned, Dr Gourvish has concluded[9] that they were unmanageable throughout most of the post-war period because of the changing and conflicting expectations of the politicians.

In 1962 the British Transport Commission was wound up, and the railways were transferred to the British Railways Board. The requirement that it should break even financially went by default, but an attempt was made to clarify the Board's financial responsibility in the Transport Act of 1968. This, following the recommendations of the Low Report of 1960,[10] was intended to relieve railway management of the need to maintain loss-making but 'socially necessary' services out of general revenue; instead, the short-fall on each such service would be identified and met from taxation. This transferred the decision to the politicians responsible for spending public money, and despite arguments about the calculation of the subvention, it was an obvious improvement. However, it proved contrary to the provisions of the Treaty of Rome, and was replaced under the Railways Act of 1974 by a blanket subsidy for the 'social railway'.

Current policy

In 1993 the government took the controversial step of breaking up British Rail and introducing private ownership. The way this was done was influenced by a 1991 Directive of the European Commission, requiring all member states to introduce commercial management, separate accounts for infrastructure and operations, and some degree of open access to their railways. Instead of just setting up separate accounts, the British government (like some others) set up a separate administration, Railtrack, for the infrastructure, and then privatised it. Train operations were then divided up as if they were separate businesses, and were offered to commercial firms by way of tender. Each of these franchises (with the exception of the Gatwick Express, which is profitable) carried with it a reducing amount of subsidy, with the ultimate objective of ending state finance to the railways. Rolling stock for passenger trains, however, was to be leased by the Train Operating Companies (TOCs). The freight business was sold off with no similar constraints, and the various engineering and other activities of the British Railways Board were sold off separately.

Road freight transport, as we have seen, was only partially nationalised in 1947, and partially denationalised by the Transport Act of 1953. In 1968 the road fleets of British Railways and British Road Services, with some other state-owned concerns, were vested in a National Freight Corporation, but the Transport Act of 1980 renamed this the National Freight Company. Again renamed a Consortium, it was later sold to its staff. Public haulage and distribution is thus today a private sector industry. While public authorities still own a good many own-account vehicles, there is no nationalised road haulage.

Freight transport and distribution by road is provided by a large number of firms, including one-man-one-truck businesses, which often work by subcontracting from larger firms. The economies of scale lie in being either small or quite large, which accounts for this pattern of ownership. There is a distinction between haulage, which, broadly, is the movement of large single consignments, and distribution, which includes parcel carriers like Royal Mail. Most of the large distribution companies work on a hub-and-spoke system, with trucks bringing their loads into the hub (usually in the Midlands) at night-time, where they are reorganised into loads to be taken on to their destination. A large number of small firms feed traffic into this movement, as well as providing local pick-up and delivery services in their own areas.

Goods vehicles of less than 3.5 tonnes gross weight are treated like private cars, with the requirement of an ordinary driver's licence, and an annual safety test (the 'MOT test') after the first three years from new. At 3.5 tonnes and over it becomes necessary for the driver to hold a Heavy Goods Vehicle (HGV) licence, subject to a strict driving test. These vehicles can only be operated by a firm or individual holding a current Operator's Licence (O-licence), incorporating standards laid down by the European Commission. A similar requirement applies to the operation of buses and coaches – Public Service

Vehicles (PSVs) – so it will be convenient to outline this system of control here. (To drive a PSV you must hold a PSV driver's licence, also subject to a strict test, although this does not apply to the light van conversions generally known as minibuses.)

Licensing control

The O-licence will be issued to an applicant who can satisfy the requirements; this is where the system differs from those designed to favour certain classes of operator. The requirements are as follows:

- to be of GOOD REPUTE;
- to have APPROPRIATE FINANCIAL STANDING;
- to show evidence of PROFESSIONAL COMPETENCE;

(in addition, for a Goods O-licence, certain environmental conditions must be satisfied).

When an application is made to the licensing authority (an official appointed by the Secretary of State for Transport), the requirements can be *discharged* in the following ways:

- as to GOOD REPUTE, account will be taken of any relevant convictions on the part of the applicant, his employees or agents, or (if the applicant is a company) the company's officers, and of the applicant's previous conduct (in any capacity) as an operator of any kind of vehicles for business purposes;
- as to APPROPRIATE FINANCIAL STANDING, it must be shown that there is sufficient working capital to ensure the establishment and proper administration of the business, and safe operation of the vehicles;
- as to PROFESSIONAL COMPETENCE, the applicant must hold, or employ as a manager someone who holds a Certificate of Professional Competence (CPC), issued after passing or having exemption from an examination conducted by the Royal Society of Arts (in the Republic of Ireland, by the Chartered Institute of Transport).

But this is not all. As well as the environmental suitability of the applicant's operating base (for the goods licence), attention has to be given to two more requirements:

■ There must be adequate facilities and arrangements for the maintenance of the vehicles in a fit and serviceable condition.
■ There must be adequate arrangements for ensuring compliance with laws relating to the driving and operation of the vehicles.

The second of these is specially concerned with the limitations laid down on the hours of work of HGV and PSV drivers.

Only when there is a favourable reaction to all these matters will the O-licence be issued, which will specify the number of vehicles that may be operated from the base. Once authorised, they can be inspected at any time, and will be subject to an annual inspection. The authority has power to reduce as well as to increase the number. Serious misbehaviour, leading to the revocation of the O-licence, means that the holder is put out of business, which is the most effective sanction for the enforcement of what is called the *quality control* of the industry.

The O-licence may be for national or for international operation, and the PSV system also has a special class for what is loosely called 'community transport'. Other than this, the goods industry is subject to no further restrictions unless the firm wishes to operate outside Great Britain.

Passenger operators require permits for much European movement, but the bus industry is also subject to further control where 'local bus services' are concerned. (These are defined as services on which it is possible for a passenger to travel a distance of less than 15 miles, at a separate fare). Anyone who holds a valid PSV O-licence may run such a service unless specifically banned from doing so; all that is necessary is to *register* certain details, such as the route and frequency (not the fares), giving 42 days' notice before starting to run. Any significant changes, including the abandonment of the service, also require 42 days' notice. This system was introduced under the Transport Act of 1985, and it is intended to enable local authorities to identify 'socially necessary' services that they can offer to the trade for tender; a policy not unlike that recommended for the railways by the Low Report, as we have already seen.

Transport Acts 1947–78

The ownership of the bus and coach industry has always been much more complex than that of goods transport. From 1916 onwards there was the development of 'area agreement' bus companies, each seeking to carve out a territorial monopoly, and the inter-war years saw these tending to combine into three major groups, while at the same time attracting up to 49 per cent shareholdings on the part of the main line railway companies. Alongside them there was a handful of substantial firms and a great many small ones that remained independent, together with the municipal transport departments, both large and small, many of them originating as tramway operators.

The nationalising Act of 1947 did not provide for the immediate transfer of the industry to the British Transport Commission, but the BTC automatically acquired the shares owned by the railways, and so became a significant stake-holder. Three of the holding companies then in existence proceeded to sell their subsidiaries to the BTC, and a three-fold division of the industry into state-owned, municipal and independent sectors emerged. Moves were made in 1950 to set up Area Boards, as provided for under the 1947 Act, but these were dropped after Labour lost the general election in the following year – and, as we have seen, they were resisted by the Labour-controlled councils of several cities. But the denationalisation of the industry did not take place, and in 1968 the situation was tidied up when the remaining group sold its interests to the state and the companies that had come into public ownership were vested in the newly formed National Bus Company and Scottish Bus Group.

At the same time there was the first major restructuring of municipal transport undertakings in their history. When Barbara Castle was Minister of Transport there had been some radical rethinking of policy, expressed in a series of White Papers that still make challenging reading. In one of these, *Public Transport and Traffic*[11] the need was expressed for land-use and transportation planning to be co-ordinated, specially in what were coming to be called the conurbations. The original conception of Conurbation Transport Authorities (CTAs) emerged however in the Transport Act of 1968 as Passenger Transport Authorities (PTAs). These had operating functions through the appointment of Passenger Transport Executives (PTEs) which were set up for the urban areas of Merseyside, Tyneside, Greater Manchester (designated South East Lancashire and North East Cheshire, or SELNEC), and the West Midlands. In each case the PTA was endowed with all the municipal bus fleets in its area (which caused no little discontent in towns like Walsall and cities like Birmingham). In some cases the operations of the local NBC company were acquired, while in others a co-ordinating agreement was made. The PTE had considerable reserve powers, and the bus operators were given a duty to co-ordinate their services with it, with each other, and with British Rail. The PTEs also received powers to subsidise public transport by road and rail.

The total effect of the 1968 Transport Act was thus to increase the centralisation of inland passenger transport. (A co-ordinating council was even provided for the state-owned freight operators, including the GPO, though it met but once, since it had no effective power.) The process was carried further by the Local Government Act of 1972, the product of a Conservative government, which gave subsidy and co-ordination powers to the so-called 'shire counties' while at the same time (almost as an after-thought) defining the new Metropolitan County Councils as PTAs under the 1968 Act. This had the effect of creating two new PTAs (West Yorkshire and South Yorkshire), and of altering the boundaries of the existing ones in ways that had little to do with the logic of public transport or planning, but much to do with the political composition of the new councils. Thus Coventry became part of the West Midlands and Southport part of Merseyside, while Tyneside became Tyne and Wear, with wide acres of green fields to be served. At the same time, the logic of giving PTA status to conurbations such as Avon or Cleveland, or the Nottingham-Mansfield-Derby triangle, did not attract the favour of the politicians.

Responsibility for London Transport, on the other hand, was accepted somewhat grudgingly by the Greater London Council under the Transport (London) Act of 1969, leading to a tragic-comic story of political intervention at the expense of good management.[12]

Scottish local government reform had rather less impact; a PTA for Greater Glasgow (renamed Strathclyde in 1980) removed operating powers from the city council, while those of the cities of Aberdeen, Dundee and Edinburgh were transferred to the new regional councils. The Act of 1968 produced a state-owned bus holding company, the Scottish Bus Group, comparable to the NBC, but the Scottish territorial bus companies had been in state ownership since 1949.

This centralisation of control over the bus industry led in the case of the shire counties to a general tendency for the co-ordinating offices appointed under the 1972 Act to acquire some of the functions of management. (This varied from 'benign neglect' in some counties to full-blooded intervention in others.) In the Metropolitan Counties, however, public transport was rapidly politicised, and the PTEs had to report to committees of the councils. The objective of co-ordinating land-use and transportation planning was if anything set back by the Local Government Act of 1972, which separated the two functions into parallel branches of the county hall bureaucracy. A White Paper in 1977[13] argued for the transfer of funds from road expenditure to the subsidy of buses, which rose in ten years from £172 million to £441 million, the greater part being applied to services operated by or on behalf of the PTEs in the Metropolitan Counties.

The radical changes of the 1980s

Throughout the period described above, and indeed since 1931, the bus and coach industry had been subject to a system of licensing that virtually prevented competition in all but the private charter of vehicles. This was exercised by area Traffic Commissioners through the requirement that all regular operations at separate fares required a road service licence (originally introduced by the Road Traffic Act of 1930). The system was swept away in two stages, by the Transport Acts of 1980 and 1985, and replaced by the O-licence and the need to register local bus services that we have already seen. This process of deregulation was feared and resisted by much of the bus industry and by most of the local politicians and administrators concerned with it, but it seems to have been judged a success, and little is heard about returning to the old monopolies. Thus the trend to centralised control may be said to have been reversed.

Still more so has it been reversed by the restructuring of the industry that formed a separate part of the Act of 1985. Not only was the National Bus Company wound up, and its subsidiaries sold (either to management teams or to private sector ownership), but the same process was followed in the case of the Scottish Bus Group and for London. (With the demise of the Greater London Council, 'London Transport' passed in 1986 to a regional body, London Regional Transport, and the buses and Underground were vested in separate subsidiary companies.) The PTE bus fleets passed to new company ownership, and while the shares in these companies remained in the ownership of the PTE, they were required to be managed commercially; the same provision was made for the bus fleets of such district councils as had inherited powers to run public transport. These 'arms-length' companies were intended to be transferred to the private sector, and most of them were; but 19 businesses remain in the ownership of municipal councils. The PTE fleets were initially the subject of employee buy-outs, but all of them have now come into the ownership of one or other of the bus industry's group holding companies.

But we have already seen that the bus operators were subject to varying intensity of political control under the 1968 and 1972 Acts, and that one of the most effective means of control lay in the use of subsidy. In some cases the bus managers progressively lost their freedom of action to policy-makers in the council offices. Of all forms of management it may be said that power flows where money flows, but by the end of the 1970s it was becoming plain that local government administrators did not always make good managers. The Transport Act of 1985 radically changed the way in which subsidy could be applied to bus services, by limiting councils to inviting tenders for the provision of socially necessary services that the new commercially driven companies did not register. When combined with the effect of 'rate-capping' on local councils, and the abolition of the Metropolitan County Councils, the decentralisation of the bus industry had been achieved.

CURRENT CONTROLS OF OTHER TRANSPORT MODES

There is less to be said about the remaining branches of inland transport. The development of pipelines is probably least known, yet the first, from Bristol to Reading, was commissioned in 1941. In 1997 they accounted for 11 per cent of the total volume of goods carried in the United Kingdom. Freight moved by water accounted for 21 per cent of the total volume, a figure that includes both inland and coastal movements. It has recently been recognised that coastwise shipping (that is, between two ports within the United Kingdom) could carry more freight, and relieve the motorways, and government grants are available for the development of terminal facilities.

Air transport

Internal air transport again represents a small proportion of the total movement, even though the published figures include travel to and from Northern Ireland and the Channel Islands (a water crossing notably attracts more traffic to air). In 1986 a mere 1 per cent of passenger kilometres used internal air service, a figure that had been constant for the previous ten years. When it is remembered that a part of this would consist of people 'interlining' (ie linking with international air services), the significance of the mode is small. The traffic is shared between British Airways and competitors, and is subject to a form of route licensing that was developed from the system abandoned for the bus industry in 1985. The Civil Aviation Authority is however rather less restrictive in its decision-making than the former bus licensing authorities were required to be.

Air transport in a country as small as ours must – at least in the present stage of technology – be linked with international demand, and here the situation becomes very much more complex. Although there has been a trend to greater commercial freedom in recent years, including extensive deregulation in the USA and Europe, the world airlines are still essentially governed by a series of agreements between individual governments as to what airlines can fly what route. Alongside this, for the formative years of international flying after the Second World War, the International Air Transport Association (IATA) operated as a world-wide organisation acting on behalf of airlines to pursue their perceived interests, not always or indeed often in the interests of their customers. The result of this structure of control has been to favour high-cost airlines at the expense of low-cost carriers, and to permit the existence of national 'flag-carriers' whose operations could not survive in a competitive market.

The central problem about the control of the international air transport industry seems to be the way it is seen as an expression of national status, and the experience of the British industry has not been free from this. Told by Winston Churchill in 1919 that they had to 'fly by themselves', infant British airlines faced subsidised competition on flights to France and Belgium, and had to be given financial support in order to survive. The government then set up Imperial Airways as its 'chosen instrument' (chosen for the receipt of subsidy), but the experiment was not a success. After a number of small companies started to fly in the 1930s a second 'chosen instrument', called British Airways, was formed in 1935, to fly internal and European services, but in 1940 the government decided to nationalise the industry, setting up the British Overseas Airways Corporation, with Sir John Reith at its head.

BOAC had a sort of shadow life while the war lasted, and then the new government reorganised the industry into three corporations – BOAC, British European Airways (BEA) and British South American Airways (BSAA, a corporation in which the shipping industry had a financial interest). BSAA proved unsuccessful in that period of financial crisis, and was wound up, but the two state-owned organisations that remained were supposed to reflect the different type of aircraft needed for short and long haul routes. In 1969 the Edwards Report[14] recommended that there should be an independent 'third force' airline, and steps were taken to create this in the shape of British Caledonian. But the logic of the Edwards Report was abandoned when BEA and BOAC were merged in 1974 to form a new British Airways, which was privatised in 1986, and which in 1988 absorbed British Caledonian's services as well.

Apart from the maintenance and administration aspects of airline management itself the infrastructure of the industry is taken care of by Air Traffic Control and by the various bodies responsible for the provision of terminals. Air Traffic Control, a sort of policing of the skies, is the responsibility of the Civil Aviation Authority, but airports are run by several different kinds of authority, one of which used to be called the British Airports Authority (but, since being privatised in 1987, prefers to be known as just BAA). BAA operates seven airports, of which Heathrow, Gatwick and Stansted are the biggest, while the others are all in Scotland. Many formerly municipally owned airports have been privatised or have a majority shareholding in the private sector. A new airport in London's Docklands was built by a major civil engineering company. There has also been some improvement to access by public transport, by rail, coach and, in Manchester and Newcastle upon Tyne, by extension of the local metro system. As well as the major airports there are many smaller ones, and a multitude of landing strips and helicopter pads, a lot of them for private or business use.

Sea transport

Seaports are similarly the responsibility of a range of different bodies, the largest of which, Associated British Ports, was privatised in 1983. Some, like Ipswich, are municipal; others, like Felixstowe, have always been privately owned. Famous names from the past, such as the Port of London Authority and the Mersey Docks and Harbours Board (now a company) have lost importance as shipping technology and the direction of British trade have changed so much. There is a complicating factor here too, since it does not follow that the seaport as a terminal and the harbour as a geographical feature (requiring conservation and navigational management) will be under the same control.

The 'policing' of the seaways is by no means as well organised as that of the airlanes, largely because the international community, acting through the International Maritime Organisation, has never been able to reach agreement about the enforcement of the rules in international waters. But the essential work of maintaining safety around our coasts is carried on by the Corporation of Trinity House, which is responsible, among other things, for the lighthouses and lightships around the coasts of England, Wales and Ireland (Scotland and the Isle of Man come under the Commissioners of Northern Lighthouses). Providing rescue services comes under a voluntary body, the Royal National Lifeboat Institution, along with the Coastguard Service, which is administered by Department of the Environment, Transport and the Regions (DETR).

Shipping itself has always been basically a commercial business, war-time emergencies apart, and the former railway 'packet boats' have long since become ferries, so that the sea crossings are just a link in the road map. The train ferries, too, have disappeared, as the Channel Tunnel made them redundant. There is a broad distinction between coastal and deep sea shipping, but since coastal includes trade with northern Europe and the Republic of Ireland, it is often subdivided to recognise *coastwise* trade (movement of ships between two British ports). This today is almost entirely made up of petrol and oil, since road or rail transport is so much more economical for other commodities. But in addition to the ferries, a great deal of freight moves across the narrow seas, and there are many small ports, such as King's Lynn, Poole and Fleetwood, that are engaged in this trade.

Deep sea shipping has changed more dramatically than any other mode in the past 50 years, first with the virtually complete loss of passenger traffic to the airlines, and then with the development of container ships to replace the old general carriers. The cruise liners remain, as do the bulk cargo tramps, but there has also been the growth of the very large bulk carriers, both for liquids like oil and material like iron ore. Along with these changes there has been a great reduction in manning levels. Because of the high standards negotiated by the trade unions concerned, the British merchant marine has been drastically reduced, from 1,977 vessels in 1970 to 392 in 1997. Part of the problem has been the growth over a long period of shipping fleets registered under 'flags of convenience', to take advantage of less demanding conditions on the register of countries like Panama and Liberia. This is now to be changed, to favour registration in the UK.

Safety at sea is a matter for the enforcement of the nations concerned, as are such matters as the provision of radio communication, cooks, nurses and doctors. Maritime insurance is also very much concerned with seaworthiness. The commercial side of the industry is a complex of ownerships, chartering and liner sailing, much of it orchestrated from London. Since the 1860s, shipping companies have sought to rationalise competition – not always in the interests of traders – through a series of 'conferences', but since 1985 the United Kingdom has subscribed to a United Nations convention designed to limit their less desirable activities.

Inland waterways

Before we conclude this survey of the nation's transport agencies, we must turn to the one mode that is now least in importance, despite its former glory; the inland waterways and canals. Compared with the mainland of Europe or the United States, Britain simply does not have the natural waterways that carry so much freight elsewhere. Our canals were almost all built to such a narrow gauge that the narrow boats could not carry on the same scale as the railways, and had largely lost their economic significance before the road transport industry was motorised. The British Waterways Board (now British Waterways) succeeded to the ownership of most of the inland canals, while various river navigation authorities maintain access to inland industry, as for example on the rivers like the Trent and the Weaver. Manchester and Gloucester are examples of ports to which access is by a ship canal, extending the Mersey in one case and the Severn in the other.

Supervising all this activity are the government departments concerned, with the Department of the Environment, Transport and the Regions (DETR) having the widest interest in all modes. Others include the Ministry of Agriculture, Fisheries and Food (fishing is, after all, a branch of the transport industry); the Board of Customs and Excise, which is much involved in both sea and air ports; the Office of Fair Trading, which has responsibilities for competition in the bus and coach industry; the Health and Safety Commission and Executive (a driver's cab, for example, is a 'place of work' under the Health and Safety at Work Act); the Home Office, through the police forces; the Department of Trade and Industry, with some interest in air transport and shipping; the Race Relations Board; the Equal Opportunities Commission; and, for certain purposes, the Scottish and Welsh Offices. Transport managers, as can be seen, have a wide variety of masters to serve.

The establishment of a Scottish Parliament and an Assembly for Wales includes the transfer of certain responsibilities for transport to these new masters. The future may hold further devolution of power within England, to regional councils of some kind. But it must be remembered that, behind all these, the European Commission exercises considerable control over all forms of transport activity, so the development of its policies for the industry and the motorist must always be allowed for.

FOOTNOTES

[1] See R H Thornton (1959), *British Shipping*, 2nd edn, Cambridge University Press, Cambridge, pp 37ff.

[2] See A J Taylor (1972), *Laissez-faire and State Intervention in Nineteenth Century Britain*, Macmillan, Basingstoke, pp 39–42.

[3] See M R Bonavia (1980), *The Four Great Railways*, David and Charles, Devon. The companies were the London and North Eastern, London Midland and Scottish Great Western, and Southern.

[4] Royal Commission on Transport, 2nd Report, Cmd. 3416, 1929, HMSO, London.

[5] See M R Bonavia (1979), *The Birth of British Rail*, George Allen and Unwin, London, pp 103–04.

[6] See D H Aldcroft (1968), *British Railways in Transition*, Macmillan, Basingstoke, pp 113–15.

[7] Transport Statistics Great Britain 1998, HMSO, London.

[8] The rapid inflation around 1980 makes later figures less significant.

[9] T R Gourvish (1986), *British Railways 1948-73: A Business History*, Cambridge University Press, Cambridge.

[10] Report from the Select Committee on Nationalised Industries upon British Railways (chaired by Sir Toby Low), HMSO, London, 1960.

[11] Cmnd. 3481, 1967.

[12] For the full story, see P E Garbutt (1985), *London Transport and the Politicians*, Ian Allan, London.

[13] Transport Policy, Cmnd. 6836 lq77.

[14] *British Air Transport in the 1970s* (1969), HMSO, London.

5

Managing the Transport Business

I am the unnoticed, the unnoticeable man:
The man who sat on your right in the morning train

Peter Black: *The Man in the Bowler Hat*

Society throughout the world is increasingly made up of people living in towns and cities. While there are good reasons for this – people generally seem to prefer it – we should stop for a moment and examine how it is that this can be possible. After all, it is as true in Latin America and China as it is in the so-called 'developed economies', and it became increasingly widespread in the course of the twentieth century.

Life in the city is entirely dependent upon three industries, none of which has a particularly high profile in people's imagination. These industries are: first, agriculture; then public health; and then, transport. Who is the figure that comes to mind when we think of each of these? For the first, the farm labourer; for the second, perhaps the dustman. And for transport, the lorry driver, or maybe the air hostess. Yet we need the increasingly complex agricultural industry to keep us alive, and without drainage and refuse disposal the doctors would be hard put to save us from disease. And without

70

transport (and communications) we could not arrive at the benefits that come from urban life. What a shame that each of these industries commands so little respect; indeed, each of them seems to many people to be boring.

Yet transport does have its fascinations. Boys and girls like playing with train sets and model car racing. And someone has observed that people are over-worked, because they all have two jobs: their own, and running the railways. Yet if the status of the transport worker is seen to be so low, the status of the transport manager has for a long time been little better. Transport is the key to the supply chain that feeds us and makes our jobs possible, and it is a challenging and ever-changing industry to work in, even though, job for job, rather better salaries can be obtained in other parts of the economy.

ENGINEERING AND TRAFFIC

There are two aspects to transport management, which must always overlap, yet which can at times seem to be in conflict. On the one hand, you have obviously got to have safety and reliability, which is where the engineering function is important; but you also have to work with staff and with customers, so as to provide the service that is required of you, at the time and place where it is needed. Failure in either of these functions cannot be accepted if the business is to survive.

One of the key problems for the manager is the nature of the transport product – it cannot be stored. If a manufacturing firm suffers a strike, it should have enough stock to go on selling its product while management sorts things out, but if a bus company or a seaport is shut down, it has nothing to sell. The same is true of all service industries, because you cannot *store* a service; it perishes in the very moment of production.

So, in a very real sense, you cannot afford to get it wrong. A valid criticism of much of railway management as late as the 1970s was that they thought they were in the business of running trains – not of carrying people and goods. This was a sort of hangover from the Railway Age, when the companies had little competition, but it also reflected the extent to which the railway industry was dominated by engineers, with commercial managers, as they used to be called, having little power and low status.

None the less, the industry in every mode is constantly driven by engineering progress. Sometimes this is highly technical, as with the jet engine, which revolutionalised civil aviation. Sometimes it is the recognition of an improved technique, like the standard container, which revolutionised shipping, road and rail transport. Yet in the bus industry, when traffic managers thought they would gain by moving the engine to the back (so as to have more seats and no need for a conductor), the engineers, with some difficulty, obliged, but the consequences do not seem to have been all that satisfactory. There have also been examples, especially in the United States, where investment in high-tech light rail schemes has been wasteful, since their commercial viability was not assessed before the decision was taken to build them.

Some of the big advances in transport have come from the insights of business managers into the potential of supplying unsatisfied demand. With the deregulation of civil aviation in the European Union has come the growth of low-cost airlines, while the privatisation of railways in Britain has been followed by a significant increase in the quantity of goods carried by train. The roll-on-roll-off ferry was invented by a shipping man, using surplus military landing craft; he was derided at the time, but the ferries are one of the success stories of the whole transport industry.

The transport manager, then, must be able to see both sides of the business. The engineer must respect the traffic people, and the traffic managers must have insight into what the engineering side can, and cannot, do. The 'tilting trains' that allow much higher speeds on inter-city railways require specially formed track from the civil engineers as well as advanced technology from the mechanical engineers – and then they must be run at the best times for the customers, and effectively marketed to the public, by the commercial side of the business.

The transport industry can be considered under two headings, and this must always be borne in mind. They are: the *infrastructure* (in railway terms, 'track, terminals and signalling'), and *movement*, or what moves on the infrastructure. At one time railway transport was unique in having both functions in the same organisation; today this exists only for tramway systems, 'heritage' lines, and one small railway in the Isle of Wight. Otherwise railway companies in Britain pay Railtrack for the use of the infrastructure, the road operators and car users pay taxes, and the government provides the track. For sea and air transport the 'track' is costless, but terminal and signalling costs, including air traffic control, have to be paid by the user. (Navigational aids at sea, such as lighthouses, are regarded as a public good, and not charged to shipowners.)

A PEOPLE BUSINESS

Transport ranks as a labour intensive industry, which means that staff at all levels are a most valuable asset. This shows up in the competition between buses, coaches, trains and even aircraft, on the one hand, and private cars on the other. If you drive your own car your labour costs are limited to some part of its maintenance, and even that you can avoid, by changing cars frequently, or doing your servicing yourself. Once you are carrying passengers, or sharing, the difference is even more marked. The same relationship applies to all forms of electronic communication, which can reduce the number of journeys required in business or private life.

All the same, there is no doubt that traffic by road, rail, air and sea will continue to expand, as long as the world's economy continues to expand, and as long as the tourism market continues to grow. And it is in the nature of the industry that it depends upon the competence of the people who work in it if it is to flourish. This is due to two things: the complexity of the machinery, and the need to look after the customer. A long-distance truck driver who forgets to check the lubrication of his vehicle can easily lead to many thousands of pounds of investment having to be written off. There are many situations in which the safety of passengers and crew in an airliner or a cruise ship depends upon the skills of the captain and the navigator. Train drivers have to know how to handle their equipment, and they also have to be trained to know the peculiarities of the route they are qualified to operate on. In comparison with this, the standards required of us to hold a driving licence are really unjustifiably low – as is slowly being recognised. For one thing, all commercial drivers in all modes are subject to limited hours of work – no car drivers are subject to this important safety requirement.

Alongside this there is the importance of the 'point-of-sale' staff; the people who are in direct contact with the customers. Civil aviation is well aware of this, with the training of cabin staff and check-in people at airports, but it is a sad comment on the bus industry that only recently have its more progressive companies started to instruct drivers in 'customer care'. Train operating companies are becoming aware of the need to ensure good standards for their conductors and booking clerks, and no doubt will do so in due course for those who make announcements over station loudspeakers. Here, as with machinery, mistakes can cost companies a lot of money, this time in lost traffic, and in discouraging new customers, who may be put off by the standards that they experience.

Point-of-sale staff such as booking clerks at railway stations work as part of a team, with supervision. Salespeople at travel agencies are not part of the management of the transport company, or even, in many cases, of the tour operator. Distribution customers usually place their orders by telephone or e-mail, and these are dealt with by staff at the customer's office; this is becoming increasingly true for train operating companies, though business bookings may be handled through an agency. All of these examples require varying types of supervision to ensure that the customer is satisfied, so that further sales can be expected. Things are different when the staff concerned are not working in the firm's offices, or perhaps at an agency.

Many of the people who are in direct contact with the public, as well as those responsible for driving expensive and complex vehicles or vessels, must be subject to *management at a distance*. Train drivers are seldom in touch with the passenger (and the tradition of thanking the engine driver when you reach the terminus seems to have been lost). But train conductors and catering staff are in direct contact with the passengers, as also are bus drivers, and the few remaining bus conductors. In an aeroplane or on a ferry there is a supervisory structure, but on buses and trains the point-of-sale staff are normally working alone.

Nor is it only on the passenger side that this state of affairs exists. Increasingly in the logistics industry firms seeking *added value* look to their drivers to provide services to customers beyond the delivery of the goods. They may be required to install and test computers or other forms of apparatus; to take new orders; or to inform customers of services offered by the company. Regulations concerning the distribution of the load over the vehicle may require the driver to relocate part of it as consignments are delivered or collected.

This last example raises further complications, because a driver whose vehicle is stopped by the police for a roadside check by the officers of the Licensing Authority will be personally responsible if the distribution is at fault. This is an absolute offence; he cannot pass the blame on to his employer. This may seem a rather extreme example of the problems of management at a distance, but it reminds us that a well-run business should be able to rely on its staff, even when they are out on the road.

This is what is involved when you are running a 'people business'. The relationships between operating staff and first-line managers – supervisors, in other words – are the key to success. Those who come into the industry as career managers, and who start in first-line positions, need to realise that they will be dealing with older people with greater knowledge and experience, and indeed much greater responsibilities. If, however, the company can become what is called a *learning organisation*, with staff at every level engaged in an acceptable plan for the pursuit of excellence, then management at a distance will no longer present the problems that can so easily arise.

LOYALTY AND MOBILITY

There was a time when someone joining a railway company expected to have a job for life, moving up the management order in due course, perhaps by nothing more than increasing seniority, and retiring with the security of a pension. Various benefits like free or reduced-price travel (which were of course taxable) went along with this, but in return there was a strong element of loyalty to 'the service', almost like belonging to a military regiment. One of the disadvantages of this for the industry was the difficulty of breaking free from the tradition of the service, and making innovative breakthroughs in management and technical performance. Under state owner- ship the growth of a bureaucratic structure of management tended to inhibit innovation still more, though with exceptions, such as the development of freightliner trains. Today's comp- anies have shown that breakthroughs can be made in an industry that must also respect the lessons of past practice, especially where safety is concerned, and a railway career is still an attractive proposition, albeit a more risky and exciting one.

The real change that has swept through the transport industry in recent years has arisen from privatisation, and, indeed, the highly competitive road freight and distribution industry has been open to new management ideas ever since it was deregulated in 1963. Air, rail and road transport comp- anies are now treated by investors as if they were like any other kind of business, and managers are judged by the firm's performance, measured generally by the return on its capital. (Shipping firms are treated in the same way, but the profession of seafaring is less likely to be affected by these changes, since, by and large, it did not experience nationalisation.)

One consequence for management and recruitment has been the increasing tendency for mid-career managers to come into transport firms from other aspects of business, such as accountancy, marketing and human relations management. Along with this has come a shift away from the job-for-life attitude that used to be common when transport was perhaps seen as more of a profession than an industry. There is much to be said for people moving around, and the good transportant should be able to contribute to the success of firms in various ways, and to bring experience in one to management in another.

This is, of course, less true for the engineering side, where technological differences between railway, airline, shipping and road transport firms are greater than differences in management style and practice. But there are basic principles that apply throughout the industry; transport law, for example, which owes its origin to maritime trading.

In all branches of the transport industry there must be representation of the staff, usually through trade unions. The Rules of Oléron in the twelfth century laid down the principle that 'cargo is the mother of wages', meaning that the crew of a vessel must complete the voyage before they can be paid off. It is this idea that makes strikes such a problem throughout the industry; as the road transport industry has it, 'you can't earn anything if the wheels aren't turning'. All of which illustrates the importance of good labour relations in the interests of everyone concerned.

The history of the industry has been marked by strikes, many of which have damaged the interests of both sides in the dispute. The railway strike of 1919 encouraged people to use the new bus services, while the national bus strike of 1958 encouraged the use of the private car. Privatisation has made it more difficult to close down an entire branch of the industry, as was attempted at one time for the docks, and today's industrial relations are more usually based on 'plant bargaining' than on a national agreement covering the whole of the country.

Loyalty and responsibility are the key to successful transport operations, and the principle of management at a distance makes the subject of labour relations central to the concerns of trade unions and management alike. This has been known in the coaching trade for many years, and it is interesting to note that coach drivers are less likely to belong to a union – or, in trade union terms, are difficult to organise.

OTHER MANAGEMENT MATTERS

Transport, as we have seen, is a fail-dangerous industry that must be subject to regulation to a greater or lesser extent. Mechanical or human failure is more likely to have serious consequences than would be likely in other occupations. Understanding the regulations and working within them takes a great deal of managers' time and attention. Keeping up to date may seem enough of a problem in itself. Not all of the regulations are easy to understand and apply – the bus and coach industry has had problems over the fitting of seat belts, and the EU regulations on road vehicle drivers' permitted hours of work were complex enough, even before the adoption of minimum wage legislation. British sea and airport authorities have to check the compliance of foreign ships and aircraft with national and international standards, and may take possession of them in cases of failure.

The larger transport companies, generally working through the trade associations, negotiate with government departments so as to make sure that the impact of regulations upon their operations is understood. The associations in turn provide their members with information and advice. But as well as regulation, there is government policy for the industry in a broader sense, especially when there is a general election followed by a change of party.

Whether we like it or not, transport is a highly political subject, and many people have confirmed ideas about how it should be run. The industry thus needs to be very good at public relations, and managers need to be in touch with the media, and willing to talk to various organisations, both local and national. Here too, the trade associations play their part, but they cannot be expected to take over the whole responsibility from the business. Nowhere is this more true than in the event of an accident; if the media report that 'no one was available at the company to comment', this will give the worst possible impression. Yet the legal implications of a statement to the press must be of overriding importance.

In such a highly complex industry there is always plenty for managers to do. Meetings with local government, with planning authorities, with air and seaport administrators, and with a wide range of other contracts, make for work that is never dull. It is demanding, but there is something about transport that gives people a satisfaction that they cannot find in other kinds of employment. At the same time, 'enthusiasm' is not enough, and a good educational background through membership of a professional institute is vitally important. And there is always something to be learnt from people who come into transport management from other types of employment. What we all need is for the rest of the world to recognise how essential the industry is to maintaining society today.

Note – Readers who would like to know more about the 'people business' should turn to *Managing People: A practical guide for line managers,* by Michael Armstrong (Kogan Page and the Industrial Society, 1998).

6

Careers in Transport

You must only accept your own road:
The strong unchanging steel rails of necessity,
The ardent power that drives you towards night and the
unknown terminus.

Vivian de Sola Pinto: In the Train

TRADE, PROFESSION OR INDUSTRY?

Some people see transport as an industry in its own right, while others would argue that it is an essential part of business logistics, or supply-chain management. It is increasingly seen as a human activity that covers all forms of movement, so that the transportant must include the private car in the definition, along with cycling, and, indeed, walking. This means we must think about the provision of the 'way' as well as the operation of vehicles, vessels and aircraft; so that, whatever aspect of transport attracts you, a broader understanding is essential for a successful career.

Towards the end of the twentieth century there was a growing practice throughout the world of commercialising sectors of the industry that had traditionally been provided by government or local government organisations. In Britain this took the form of privatisation, first of bus services and then of the railway business. (Road goods transport had been privatised and deregulated at intervals between 1953 and 1968.) Within the European Union civil aviation has been opened to market forces, and pressure continues to be brought to bear on countries that still have state-owned airlines to privatise them. There is similar pressure to allow various train operating companies (passenger and freight) to have access to national railway systems.

The consequence of these trends has been to restore the industry to the status of a business, firms being dependent upon profit to remain in existence, and with the pressures to achieve financial targets that investors always require. Revenue comes from the customers, together with a limited amount of subsidy from the state, largely for the provision of services that are deemed to be socially necessary, but that are not provided in the market. (These are invariably passenger services, although the government makes grants available for the improvement of rail infrastructure, and, of course, the roads are provided at public expense.)

Yet, as we have seen, transport is a 'fail-dangerous' activity, and this means that standards of quality must be maintained. So a small firm, in road haulage or the coach trade for example, has the same professional standards to look to, within its own function, as must apply to an airline or a train operating company. In this way it is still correct to see transport as a profession, and one that you can be proud to belong to. This was recognised when the Institute of Transport was founded in 1919, and today, as the Institute of Logistics and Transport, it has a status superior to that of the trade associations that are to be found in each branch of the industry.

The engineering side of the industry, and the area of accountancy, require appropriate professional standards of their own, while commercialisation has raised the status of marketing, and training is increasingly important. These are examples of professions whose members play an important part in the provision of transport, and they can offer a way of entering the industry. But for many who look to a transport career, direct entry will be more attractive.

GETTING INTO TRANSPORT

There are numerous ways of making a career in the transport industry, but there is always the need to understand it, for which this book is designed to be an introduction. Not a few people have started by getting a job as a bus or truck driver, or in a similar position in another mode of transport. There is little in the way of a formal structure today, and while merchant shipping has its cadets, and many large firms seek trainees, a job with a local small business may equally well open the door to a career.

But the more you know about the industry, the better will be your chances, which is why many people choose to take a university degree, either in the field of transport studies, or in a more general area such as business studies or accountancy, where there are transport-related options. Supply management and logistics are good examples. Other people may choose a course in the field of engineering or of town planning. Probably the best way of developing your knowledge of the industry is to find a sandwich course with a placement element, which will give you a head start in developing your career.

Most specialist degrees offer exemptions from the examinations of the professional institutes, while more general courses will probably give partial exemption. For people coming afresh to the transport industry (which is frequently the case), a professional course, perhaps by distance learning, is a good way of getting the background understanding that is so important. Alternatively (and especially for a career in planning or consultancy), a postgraduate degree in the transport field will suit the generalist graduate.

But the possession of a degree is no guarantee of a brilliant career, and some people have started by working as a driver or a receptionist, and have built up their skills from their experience. National Vocational Qualifications (NVQs) have been developed by lead bodies in the industry, and NVQ5, which extends the measure of competence to knowledge-based assessment, is the foundation for managerial responsibility. Distance learning courses for the professional institutions, or those requiring day release or block release, provide similar support to career development. Some of these may also be helpful for those with a university degree in a non-transport field.

WHAT YOU NEED TO DO WELL

There is still one factor that matters a lot in the choice of a transport career, and managers throughout the industry will be well aware of it. It is a strong identification with transport, and often with a particular mode, which may provide a motivation as great as that which takes people into medicine (or perhaps even the church!). This is not the same thing as the sometimes over-emotional devotion of the enthusiast – although many transport managers *are* themselves enthusiasts, and are happy to support the enthusiast organisations and heritage societies. Rather, as we have seen, it is a quality called *flair*, which complements and extends management competence, and which has played an important part in many a senior manager's contribution.

Flair may give useful insights into the various modes of transport, but in the end it seems to be closely related to one or another of them. There are examples of people moving from, say, shipping to railway management, but the early experiences of the bus companies that took over railway franchises were not all satisfactory. Belonging to a professional organisation, where you can meet people from other transport businesses, can help, and it is important to keep up to date by reading the trade and professional journals. Above all, if you find transport boring, then it is not a career for you.

There is, though, one thing about the business that is central to its success, and to yours if you work in it. The purpose of any form of transport is the movement of people or goods, from where they are to where they want to be, or where they should be sent. There is obviously no purpose in moving goods unless they will be worth more at the destination, and very few people make a journey just for the sake of it. Of course, the railway manager must be good at running trains, and the engineer must be devoted to his machinery so that the ship can sail safely, but running buses or trucks or aircraft empty is not good for the firm or for the economy. This is an illustration of the difference between the enthusiast, and the person with this quality we call flair. And it is the basis for something more than a satisfactory career in the transport industry; one that is satisfying as well.

Appendix 1: Transport Further/ Higher Education Courses

Reproduced from *Careers on the Move 1998–1999* by kind permission of the Chartered Institute of Transport in the UK

The data listed here represent selected extracts from the ECCTIS *computerised information service. These records have been created specifically for* Careers on the Move *by ECCTIS 2000 Limited.*

ECCTIS has been designed to give the widest possible information on the opportunities available to people applying for a place in higher or further education at any stage, and regardless of the starting point.

It is possible to select courses which are available by full and part-time study or distance learning and sandwich courses which include industrial placements.

For those who do not have or intend to gain A levels or equivalent, *ECCTIS* carries information on over 1,000 access courses.

Details of educational CATS at higher education institutions, and how they operate, are given as well as information on levels and credits assigned to specific courses, where this is available.

ECCTIS is available by subscription on CD ROM. It can already be found at over 6,500 access points both in the UK and abroad, in schools, careers offices, colleges of further education, higher education institutions, adult guidance centres and libraries. ECCTIS on CD ROM is also carrying increasing information on professional qualifications and how to acquire them.

COLLABORATION WITH *CAREERS ON THE MOVE*

An attempt to reproduce details of all transport-specific and related courses held in the extensive ECCTIS database would have been impossible, so a decision had to be taken to feature transport-specific courses only.

There are however also a great many courses which feature comprehensive and highly practical transport-allied study options, for instance many community work, geography and urban studies syllabuses. In addition, within many general and combined studies courses, there may be transport-specific specialisations, for instance the law of business and carriage, engineering, transport computing and statistics. Check the syllabus details carefully. You will be surprised where the subject of transport crops up!

One word of warning: if you find that a course does offer a transport-related option, you must check the availability of this selection. Provision often depends on the number of people wishing to take the option, and the organisation of the timetable. A bit of checking in advance could avoid disappointment.

The data reproduced here represent a selection of what is available. Some courses may not have been included because their title does not immediately suggest a relevance to this handbook.

For access to many detailed syllabuses and for further information, you can get in direct contact with: ECCTIS 2000 Ltd, Oriel House, Oriel Road, Cheltenham, Gloucestershire GL50 1XP (tel: 01242 252627; fax: 01242 258600).

HOW TO USE *CAREERS ON THE MOVE/ECCTIS* LISTINGS

The selected data are presented by transport category, eg air transport, logistics. Within the categories, the education levels used are post-graduate, undergraduate, HND and equivalent, and further education, and within these the establishments are grouped alphabetically according to location.

The addresses and telephone/facsimile numbers for the establishments are then listed.

AIR TRANSPORT (INCL. AERONAUTICS, AIRPORT PLANNING, AVIATION)

Postgraduate

Cranfield University
Department: College of Aeronautics
Duration: MPhil: 1 year full-time; PhD: 3 years full-time
Course Title: MPhil/PhD in Aeronautics
Duration: 1 year full-time or 2 to 4 years part-time
Course Title: MSc in Air Transport Management
Duration: 1 year full-time
Course Title: MSc in Astronautics and Space Engineering

University of Hertfordshire
Department: University Observatory, Division of Physical Sciences
Duration: 3 years part-time
Course Title: MSc in Astronomy/Astronautics

Loughborough University
Department: Aeronautical and Automotive Engineering and Transport Studies
Duration: 1 year full-time or 2 to 8 years part-time
Course Title: MSc in Airport Planning and Management

University of Southampton
Department: Aeronautics and Astronautics
Duration: PhD: 3 years full-time
Course Title: MPhil/PhD in Aeronautics and Astronautics

Undergraduate

City University
Department: Mechanical Engineering and Aeronautics
Duration: 4 years full-time/5 years sandwich
Course Title: MEng (Hons) in Air Transport Engineering
Duration: 4 years full-time including foundation year

Course Title: BEng (Hons) in Air Transport Engineering (with a foundation year)
Duration: 3 years full-time/4 years sandwich
Course Title: BEng (Hons) in Air Transport Engineering

North East Wales Institute
Department: Engineering
Duration: 3 years full-time or 4 years part-time
Course Title: BEng (Hons) in Aircraft/Transport Management

University of Kent
Department: School of Physical Sciences
Duration: 4 years full-time with time abroad/4 years full-time
Course Title: MPhys (Hons) in Physics with Space Science and Systems
Duration: 4 years full-time with time abroad/3 years full-time
Course Title: BSc (Hons) in Physics with Space Science and Systems

University of Leicester
Department: Physics and Astronomy
Duration: 4 years full-time
Course Title: MPhys in Physics with Space Science and Technology
Duration: 3 years full-time or 4 years full-time including foundation year
Course Title: BSc (Hons) in Physics with Space Science and Technology

HND and equivalent

East Surrey College
Department: Aviation and Engineering
Course Title: NVQ in Engineering and Aviation (Level 4)
Air Service Training (Engineering) Ltd
Duration: Open learning
Course Title: NVQ in Piloting Transport Aircraft (Level 4)

Further education

Castlereagh College of Further Education
Department: Technology
Duration: 1 to 2 years part-time evening only
Course Title: Certificate in Aviation: Licence Without Type Rating

East Surrey College
Department: Aviation and Engineering
Course Title: NVQ in Engineering and Aviation (Levels 1, 2 and 3)

Duration: 1 year part-time day, evening or open learning
Course Title: C&G-728 1 in Aviation Studies
Course Title: C&G-7280 3 in Aviation Studies: Air Transport Economics
Course Title: C&G-7280 4 in Aviation Studies: Aircraft Technology
Course Title: C&G-7280 5 in Aviation Studies: Airport Operations
Course Title: C&G-7280 2 in Aviation Studies: Operation and Flight Dispatch
Course Title: Licence without Type Rating in Civil Aviation Studies
Duration: 2 years full-time
Course Title: C&G Award in Airline Studies

London Guildhall University
Department: Civil Aviation
Duration: various 8–12 weeks
Course Title: Licence in Commercial Pilot Studies
Course Title: Licence in Private Pilot Ground Studies
Course Title: Licence in Airline Transport Pilot Studies
Course Title: Licence in Private Pilot Studies: Instrument Rating
Course Title: Licence in Private Pilot: Instrument Meteorological Conditions Rating Studies

Macclesfield College
Department: Technology
Duration: 1 year part-time evening
Course Title: Licence without Type Rating in Airframes, Engines, Electrical and Instruments

Open Learning Centre International
Duration: Open learning
Course Title: C&G-7280 05 in Aviation: Airport Operations
Course Title: NVQ in Aviation Engineering (Level 3)
Course Title: C&G-7280 in Aviation: Operations/Flight Dispatch

Oxford Air Training School
Duration: 48 weeks full-time
Course Title: Licence in Commercial Pilot (Helicopters)
Duration: Part-time
Course Title: Licence in Private Pilot (Helicopters)
Course Title: Licence in Private Pilot and Associated Rating (Fixed Wing)
Duration: 56 weeks full-time
Course Title: Licence in Commercial Pilot/Airline Transport Pilot (Aeroplanes)

Air Service Training (Engineering) Ltd
Duration: various

Course Title: Licence in Airline Transport Pilot
Course Title: Diploma in English for Foreign Students, Specialising in Aviation English
Course Title: Licence in Commercial Pilot (Aeroplanes)
Course Title: Licence in Private Pilot (Aeroplanes)

INTERNATIONAL TRANSPORT

Postgraduate

London Guildhall University
Department: Business Studies
Duration: MSc: 1 year full-time or 2 years part-time
Course Title: MSc/PgDip/PgCert in International Trade and Transport

Nottingham Trent University
Department: Civil and Structural Engineering
Duration: 2½ years distance learning
Course Title: MSc in European Traffic and Transportation

University of Plymouth
Department: Institute of Marine Studies
Duration: 12 months full-time
Course Title: MSc in International Shipping/International Logistics
Duration: 9 months full-time
Course Title: Diploma in Professional Studies in International Shipping and Logistics Management

Southampton Institute
Course Title: MBA in International Transport and Logistics

University of Westminster
Department: Transport Studies Group
Duration: 1 year full-time
Course Title: MSc in European Transport and Logistics

Undergraduate

University of Wales, Cardiff
Department: Maritime Studies and International Transport
Duration: 4 years sandwich/3 years full-time
Course Title: BSc (Hons) in International Transport

University of Huddersfield
Department: Transport and Logistics
Duration: 3 years full-time or 4 years sandwich with time abroad
Course Title: BSc (Hons) in European Logistics Management

Southampton Institute
Department: Maritime Management
Duration: 3 years full-time or 4 years sandwich
Course Title: BSc (Hons) in International Transport Management

HND and equivalent

Southampton City College
Duration: 1 year full-time
Course Title: BSc (Hons) (Foundation) in International Transport

Further education

Motherwell College
Department: Automobile Engineering
Duration: 11 weeks part-time evenings only
Course Title: Certificate of Professional Competence in Road Transport
(International)

LOGISTICS (INCL. DISTRIBUTION)

Postgraduate

University of Bath
Duration: 2 years modular part-time
Course Title: MSc in Management of Supply

University of Central England
Duration: MPhil/PhD: full-time or part-time
Course Title: MPhil/PhD in Supply Chain Management
Duration: MSc: 1 year full-time or 2 years part-time or 3 years part-time
evening only
Course Title: MSc/PgDip/PgCert in Industrial Logistics (Supply Chain
Management)/(Customer Focused Logistics)

Cranfield University
Department: School of Management: Centre for Logistics and Transportation
Duration: 2 years part-time
Course Title: MSc in Distribution and Logistics
Course Title: MPhil/PhD in Management Studies (Logistics and Distribution Systems)/(Marketing and Logistics)
Department: School of Management
Duration: 1 year full-time
Course Title: MSc in Logistics and Transportation
Department: Defence Management and Security Analysis
Duration: MSc: 47 weeks full-time
Course Title: MSc/PgDip in Defence Logistics Management
Duration: PhD: 3 years full-time
Course Title: MPhil/PhD in Defence Management (Human Relations or Procurement and Logistics)

University of East London
Department: Postgraduate Programme Area
Duration: 1 year full-time or 2 years part-time
Course Title: MSc in Logistics

University of Edinburgh
Department: Business Studies
Duration: MSc: 12 months full-time
Course Title: MSc/PgDip in Logistics and Supply Chain Management

University of Exeter
Department: Research Centre MIRCE
Duration: 3 years part-time
Course Title: MSc In Logistics Engineering

Glasgow Caledonian University
Department: Mathematics
Duration: MSc: 1 year full-time or 2 years part-time or 3 years part-time
Course Title: MSc/PgDip in Logistics

Heriot-Watt University
Department: Business Organisation, School of Management
Duration: 1 year full-time
Course Title: MSc in Logistics and Supply Chain Management

University of Huddersfield
Department: Transport and Logistics
Duration: 2 years part-time
Course Title: MSc in Transport and Logistics Management

University of North London
Duration: MPhil: full-time or part-time: PhD: full-time or part-time
Course Title: MPhil/PhD in Transport and Logistics
Duration: MA: 1 year full-time or 2 years part-time
Course Title: MA/PgDip in Supply Chain Management

University of Plymouth
Department: Institute of Marine Studies
Duration: 12 months full-time
Course Title: MSc in International Shipping/International Logistics
Duration: 9 months full-time
Course Title: Diploma in Professional Studies in International Shipping and Logistics Management

The Robert Gordon University
Department: Aberdeen Business School
Duration: MSc: 1 year full-time or 2 years part-time
Course Title: MSc/PgDip/PgCert in Purchasing and Supply Chain Management
Course Title: MSc/PgDip/PgCert in Logistics

University of Salford
Department: Management School
Duration: MSc: 2 years part-time evening; PgDip: 2 years part-time evening
Course Title: MSc/PgDip in Transport and Logistics Management
Duration: MSc: 12 months full-time or 2 years part-time evening; PgDip: 2 years part-time evening or 8 months full-time
Course Title: MSc/PgDip in Purchasing and Logistics Management

Southampton Institute
Course Title: MBA in International Transport and Logistics

Staffordshire University
Department: Postgraduate Administration
Duration: MSc: part-time evening; Diploma: part-time; Certificate: part-time
Course Title: MSc/Diploma/Certificate in Procurement and Logistics

University of Surrey
Duration: MSc: 1 year full-time or 2 years distance learning or 2 years part-time
Course Title: MSc/PgDip in Logistics and Operations Management

University of Westminster
Department: Transport Studies Group
Duration: 1 year full-time
Course Title: MSc in European Transport and Logistics

Undergraduate

Aston University
Department: Civil and Mechanical Engineering
Duration: 3 years full-time
Course Title: BSc (Hons) in Logistics (full-time)
Duration: 4 years sandwich
Course Title: BSc (Hons) in Logistics (sandwich)

Buckinghamshire College
Duration: BA: 4 years sandwich with time abroad; BA (Hons): 4 years
sandwich with time abroad
Course Title: BA/BA (Hons) in Business Studies with Logistics
Duration: 3 years full-time
Course Title: BA (Hons) in Business Administration with Logistics

Cranfield University
Department: Defence Management and Security Analysis
Duration: 3 years full-time
Course Title: MSc (Hons) in Management and Logistics

University of Glamorgan
Department: Business School
Duration: 4 years sandwich
Course Title: BA (Hons) in Purchasing and Supply Chain Management

University of Huddersfield
Department: Transport and Logistics
Duration: 4 years sandwich
Course Title: BSC (Hons) in Transport and Logistics Management
Course Title: BSc (Hons) in Logistics and Supply Chain Management
Duration: 3 years full-time or 4 years sandwich with time abroad
Course Title: BSc (Hons) in European Logistics Management
Duration: 4 years sandwich
Course Title: BSc (Hons) in Food Supply Chain Management

London Guildhall University
Department: Business Studies
Duration: BA: 4 years sandwich or 5 to 6 years part-time day or 5 to 6
years part-time evening: BA (Hons): 4 years sandwich or 5 to 6 years
part-time day or 5 to 6 years part-time evening only
Course Title: BA/BA (Hons) in Business Studies

University of Northumbria
Duration: 1 year full-time
Course Title: BA (Hons) in Logistics and Supply Chain Management

Sheffield Hallam University
Department: Combined Studies Programme
Duration: BSc: 3 years full-time or part-time day or evening; BSc
(Hons): 3 years full-time or part-time day or evenings; BA: 3 years full-time or part-time day or evening; BA (Hons): 3 years full-time or part-time day or evening
Course Title: BSc/BSc (Hons)/BA/BA (Hons) in Combined Studies

University of Ulster
Department: Campus: Jordanstown
Duration: 4 years sandwich
Course Title: BSc (Hons) in Transport and Logistics

HND and equivalent

Belfast Institute of Further and Higher Education
Department: School of Leisure Studies and Recreational Activities
Duration: 3 years full-time
Course Title: HND in Distribution
Duration: 2 years part-time day
Course Title: HNC in Distribution

Bolton College
Department: Business and Administration Sector
Duration: 2 years part-time day-release or 2 years part-time evening
Course Title: HNC in Business and Distribution

Manchester College of Arts and Technology
Department: Business Studies
Duration: 3 years part-time evening only
Course Title: Diploma in Distribution Studies
Duration: 2 years part-time day
Course Title: HNC in Distribution Studies

Milton Keynes College
Department: Logistics, Manufacturing and Professional Studies
Duration: 2 years part-time evening
Course Title: Diploma in Logistics

Motherwell College
Department: Integrated Engineering Services
Duration: 1 year full-time or 2 years part-time day-release
Course Title: HNC in Logistic Operations

University of North London
Duration: 2 years part-time day and evening or 2 years part-time
evening only or full-time
Course Title: DipHE in Purchasing and Logistics

Oxford College of Further Education
Department: Business Studies
Duration: 2 years part-time day or evening
Course Title: HNC in Distribution

South Birmingham College
Department: Management, Professional Studies and Office Technology
Duration: 2 years part-time day
Course Title: Diploma in Logistics

Stoke-on-Trent College
Department: Management
Duration: 36 weeks part-time evening
Course Title: Diploma in Logistics Management

Teesside Tertiary College
Department: General Education and Media
Duration: 1 year full-time
Course Title: HNC in Distribution

Further education

Milton Keynes College
Department: Logistics, Manufacturing and Professional Studies
Duration: 2 years full-time
Course Title: Advanced GNVQ in Logistics
Duration: 1 year part-time evening
Course Title: Certificate in Logistics

South Birmingham College
Department: Management, Professional Studies and Office Technology
Duration: 36 weeks part-time evening only
Course Title: Foundation in Logistics
Duration: 2 years part-time day
Course Title: Certificate in Logistics

Stoke-on-Trent College
Department: Management
Duration: 36 weeks part-time evening
Course Title: Foundation Certificate in Logistics
Course Title: Certificate in Logistics

West Cumbria College
Department: Business and Management
Duration: Distance learning
Course Title: Foundation Course in Logistics

West Suffolk College
Department: Humanities, Leisure and Retail Services
Duration: 1 year distance learning or 1 year part-time day or evening
Course Title: Foundation in Logistics (Level 3)
Course Title: Certificate in Logistics (Level 4)

MARITIME STUDIES (INCL. ADMINISTRATION, ENGINEERING, LAW, NAVIGATION, PORT ADMINISTRATION)

Postgraduate

University of Wales, Cardiff
Department: Maritime Studies and International Transport
Duration: 1 year full-time
Course Title: LLM in Legal Aspects of Marine Affairs
Course Title: MSc in Marine Policy
Duration: 9 months full-time
Course Title: Diploma in Port and Shipping Administration

City University
Department: Civil Engineering/Ocean Engineering Research Centre
Duration: 1 to 4 years full-time or 1 to 4 years part-time
Course Title: MPhil/PhD in Ocean Engineering

Cranfield University
Department: School of Industrial and Manufacturing Science
Duration: 1 year full-time
Course Title: MSc in Marine Technology: Underwater
Technology/Subsea Engineering/Offshore Engineering/Reliability
Engineering and Risk Management
Duration: MPhil: 1 year full-time or 2 years part-time; PhD; 3 years full-time or 4 to 6 years part-time
Course Title: MPhil/PhD in Marine Technology

University of Glasgow
Department: Naval Architecture and Ocean Engineering
Duration: MSc: 1 year part-time; PhD: 3 years part-time
Course Title: MSc/PhD in Naval Architecture and Ocean Engineering
Duration: 1 year full-time
Course Title: Diploma in Naval Architecture and Ocean Engineering

Heriot-Watt University
Department: Civil and Offshore Engineering
Duration: MSc: 12 months full-time or 2 years part-time
Course Title: MSc/Diploma in Subsea Engineering
Course Title: MSc/Diploma in Marine Resource Development and Protection

University of Hull
Duration: MSc: full-time or part-time
Course Title: MSc/PgDip in Management and Fisheries Technology

Liverpool John Moores University
Department: School of Engineering and Technology Management
Course Title: MPhil/PhD in Mechanical Marine Aeronautical, Manufacturing and Offshore Engineering
Duration: MSc: 1 year full-time or 2 years part-time; PgDip: 1 year full-time or 2 years part-time
Course Title: MSc/PgDip in Maritime Operations

London City College
Course Title: MBA in Maritime Management

University of Newcastle upon Tyne
Department: Marine Technology
Duration: MPhil: 12 months full-time or 24 months part-time; PhD: 36 months full-time or 60 months part-time
Course Title: MPhil/PhD in Marine Technology
Duration: 9 months full-time
Course Title: Certificate in Marine Engineering
Duration: 12 months full-time
Course Title: MRes in Marine Technology
Course Title: MSc in Marine Technology
Course Title: MSc in Marine Engineering

University of Nottingham
Department: Institute of Engineering Surveying and Space Geodesy
Duration: 1 year full-time or 3 years part-time
Course Title: MSc in Navigation Technology

Petroleum & Energy Studies College
Duration: Distance learning or part-time
Course Title: Postgraduate Diploma in Management of Marine Transportation of Crude Oil and Products

University of Plymouth
Department: Institute of Marine Studies
Duration: MPhil: full-time or part-time; PhD: full-time or part-time
Course Title: MPhil/PhD in Marine Studies

The University of St Andrews
Department: Scottish Institute of Maritime Studies
Duration: MPhil: 2 years full-time or part-time; PhD: 3 years full-time
or part-time
Course Title: MPhil/PhD in Maritime Studies
Duration: MPhil: 2 years full-time; MLitt: 1 year full-time
Graduate Diploma: 1 year full-time
Course Title: MPhil/MLitt/Graduate Diploma in Maritime Studies

Southampton Institute
Duration: 1 year full-time or 2 years part-time
Course Title: MSc in Marine Engineering

University of Southampton
Department: Ship Science
Duration: 12 months full-time or part-time
Course Title: MSc/Diploma in Ocean Engineering Science
Course Title: MSc/Diploma in Marine Engineering

University of Strathclyde
Department: Ship and Marine Technology
Duration: MPhil: 12 to 24 months full-time; PhD: 36 months full-time
Course Title: MPhil/PhD in Shipbuilding and Marine Technology
Duration: MSc: 12 months full-time or 24 months full-time or 24
months part-time; PgDip: 21 months part-time or 9 months full-time
Course Title: MSc/PgDip in Marine Technology

University College London
Duration: MSc: 12 months full-time or 24 months full-time; PgDip: 1
year full-time
Course Title: MSc/Graduate Diploma in Marine Engineering
Course Title: PgDip in Shipping Law
Course Title: MSc/Graduate Diploma in Ocean and Subsea
Engineering
Duration: MPhil: full-time or part-time; PhD: 3 years full-time or part-
time
Course Title: MPhil/PhD in Ocean Engineering/Naval Architecture/
Mechanical Engineering

Undergraduate

University of Wales, Cardiff
Department: Maritime Studies and International Transport
Duration: 3 years full-time/4 years sandwich
Course Title: BSc (Hons) in Maritime Studies

Cornwall College
Duration: 3 years full-time
Course Title: BSc in Marine Studies (Stage 1 modules)

Glasgow College of Nautical Studies
Duration: 3 years full-time
Course Title: BSc (Hons) in Maritime Studies

University of Glasgow
Department: Naval Architecture and Ocean Engineering
Duration: 5 years full-time
Course Title: MEng (Hons) in Naval Architecture with Fast Ship Design
Duration: 5 years full-time with time abroad
Course Title: MEng (Hons) in Naval Architecture and Ocean
Engineering with European Studies
Duration: 4 years full-time
Course Title: BEng (Hons) in Naval Architecture and Ocean
Engineering
Duration: 5 years full-time
Course Title: MEng (Hons) in Offshore Engineering
Course Title: MEng (Hons) in Naval Architecture and Marine
Engineering

Liverpool John Moores University
Department: School of Engineering
Duration: 3 years full-time/4 years full-time including foundation year
Course Title: BTech in Maritime Engineering
Course Title: BSc in Marine Operations
Course Title: BEng (Hons) in Mechanical and Marine Engineering
(Foundation)
Duration: BSc: 3 years full-time or 4 years sandwich; BSc (Hons): 3
years full-time or 4 years sandwich
Course Title: BSc/BSc (Hons) in Maritime Technology/Business
Management/Studies
Course Title: BSc/BSc (Hons) in Maritime and Intermodal Transport
Duration: BEng: 3 years full-time or 4 years sandwich; BEng (Hons): 3
years full-time or 4 years sandwich
Course Title: BEng/BEng (Hons) in Mechanical and Marine
Engineering

University of Liverpool
Department: Mechanical Engineering
Duration: 3 years full-time
Course Title: BEng (Hons) in Mechanical Engineering with Maritime
and Offshore Engineering

University of Newcastle upon Tyne
Department: Marine Technology
Duration: 3 years full-time/4 years including foundation year
Course Title: BEng (Hons) in Marine Engineering

University of Plymouth
Department: Marine Studies
Duration: 3 years full-time or 5 years part-time day
Course Title: BSc (Hons) in Marine Navigation
Course Title: BEng (Hons) in Marine Systems Technology
Course Title: BSc (Hons) in Marine Technology/Marine Studies/
Maritime Business

Southampton Institute
Duration: 3 years full-time or 4 years full-time including foundation
year
Course Title: BEng (Hons) in Maritime Technology

University of Southampton
Department: Ship Science
Duration: 4 years full-time
Course Title: MEng in Ship Science/Multidisciplinary/Naval
Architecture/Advanced Materials
Duration: 4 years full-time with time abroad
Course Title: MEng in Ship Science with European Studies
Duration: 3 years full-time or 4 years full-time including foundation
year
Course Title: BEng (Hons) in Ship Science

University of Surrey
Department: Mechanical Engineering
Duration: BEng (Hons): 4 years sandwich/3 years full-time; MEng: 4½
years sandwich
Course Title: BEng (Hons)/MEng in Mechanical Engineering with
Offshore and Maritime Engineering

University College London
Department: Mechanical Engineering
Duration: 3 years full-time or 4 years sandwich
Course Title: BEng (Hons) in Naval Architecture and Ocean
Engineering

HND and equivalent

Eastleigh College
Duration: 1 year full-time
Course Title: BEng (Hons) (Foundation) in Maritime Technology

Glasgow College of Nautical Studies
Department: Marine and Mechanical Engineering
Duration: 39 weeks full-time or distance learning
Course Title: Certificate of Competency in Marine Engineer Officer
(Class 1 and 2 Part A or B)
Duration: 2 years full-time
Course Title: HND in Marine Engineering
Course Title: HND in Maritime Studies (International Shipping
Business)

Liverpool John Moores University
Department: School of Engineering
Duration: 3 years full-time including foundation year
Course Title: HND in Marine Technology (with a Foundation Year)
Course Title: HND in Maritime Engineering (with a Foundation Year)
Duration: 2 to 3 years full-time or 2 to 3 years part-time day
Course Title: HND in Marine Technology (Seafaring)
Duration: 2 to 3 years full-time or 2 to 3 years sandwich
Course Title: HND in Marine Operations

London City College
Duration: 6 months full-time
Course Title: Diploma in Shipping Management
Duration: 9 months full-time
Course Title: Postgraduate Diploma in Shipping Management

London Guildhall University
Department: Business Studies
Duration: 1 year full-time
Course Title: University CertHE in Commercial Operation of Shipping
Studies

North Atlantic Fisheries College
Department: Marine Engineering
Duration: 1 year full-time
Course Title: HNC in Marine Engineering

Salisbury College
Duration: 1 year full-time
Course Title: BEng (Hons) (Foundation) in Maritime Technology

South Tyneside College
Department: Marine Division
Duration: 12 to 24 weeks full-time
Course Title: Certificate of Competency in Marine Engineer Officer
(Class 1)

Duration: HND: 3 years sandwich; NVQ: 3 years sandwich
Course Title: HND/NVQ in Marine Vessel Engineering (Cadet Training) (Level 3)
Duration: 3 years sandwich
Course Title: HND in Merchant Vessel Technology
Duration: 12 to 24 weeks full-time
Course Title: Certificate of Competency in Marine Engineer Officer (Class 2)

Southampton Institute
Department: Merchant Vessel Engineering
Duration: 3 years sandwich
Course Title: HND in Marine Engineering
Duration: 1 year full-time
Course Title: BEng (Hons) (Foundation) in Maritime Technology
Course Title: BSc (Hons) (Foundation) in Maritime Studies

Southampton City College
Department: Technology
Duration: 1 year full-time
Course Title: BEng (Hons) (Foundation) in Maritime Technology

Southport College
Department: Technology
Duration: 1 year full-time
Course Title: BEng Foundation in Mechanical and Marine Engineering
Duration: 3 years full-time including foundation year
Course Title: HND in Marine Technology (with a Foundation Year)

Further education

Berkshire College of Agriculture
Department: Marine Engineering
Duration: 2 years
Course Title: National Diploma in Marine Engineering
Duration: 1 year part-time
Course Title: NVQ in Marine Engineering (Level 2)

Cornwall College
Duration: 2 years full-time
Course Title: National Diploma in Maritime Technology

Liverpool John Moores University
Department: School of Engineering
Duration: Open learning
Course Title: Certificates in Marine Engineering

North West Kent College
Department: Marine Studies
Duration: 13 weeks full-time
Course Title: Certificate in Marine Engineering

South Tyneside College
Department: Marine Division
Duration: 1 term full-time
Course Title: Certificate of Competency in Marine Engineer Officer
(Class 4) (Level 3)
Duration: 3½ years sandwich
Course Title: NVQ in Merchant Vessel Operations and Merchant Vessel
Engineering (Marine Cadet) (Level 3)
Duration: 12 weeks full-time
Course Title: Certificate of Competency in Marine Engineer Officer
(Class 3)

Southampton City College
Department: Technology
Duration: 2 years part-time day
Course Title: National Certificate in Marine Technology
Duration: 2 years full-time
Course Title: National Diploma in Marine Technology

RAIL TRANSPORT

Postgraduate

The University, Sheffield
Course Title: MSc/Diploma in Rail Systems Engineering

University of York
Department: History
Duration: Diploma: part-time; MA: full-time
Course Title: MA/Diploma in Railway Studies
Course Title: MPhil/DPhil in Railway Studies

Further education

City of Westminster College
Duration: Part-time day or part-time evening only
Course Title: NVQ in Rail Transportation (Level 2)

East Surrey College
Department: Transport
Duration: 36 weeks part-time day
Course Title: C&G-738 1–2 in Railway Studies and Advanced Railway
Studies

ROAD TRANSPORT

Postgraduate

Manchester College of Arts
Duration: 1 year part-time day
Course Title: Advanced Certificate in Road Safety (MInstRS)

HND and equivalent/Further education

Because of the number of colleges which offer CPCs in road freight and
road passenger transport, it would be impractical to list them here. There
is bound to be one near where you live, so look in your local *Yellow Pages*
and contact them to find out about availability of courses. Similarly, if
you are interested in courses for the professional examinations of the
Institute of Road Transport Engineers, contact the institute direct.

TOURISM

Postgraduate

Birmingham College of Food, Tourism and Creative Studies
Department: Management and Professional Development Centre
Course Title: MA/PgDip/PgCert in Tourism Business Administration
Course Title: BPhil in Tourism Management

University of Birmingham
Department: Centre for Urban & Regional Studies
Course Title: MSc/PgDip in Leisure and Tourism Policy and Practice
Course Title: MSc/PgDip in Tourism: Policy and Management
Course Title: MPhil/PhD in Tourism: Policy and Management
Course Title: MSC/MPhil/PhD in Leisure Services and Tourism

Bournemouth University
Course Title: MA/MSc/PgDip in Tourism and Hospitality
Management

Course Title: MPhil/PhD in Service Industries and Tourism and Hospitality
Course Title: MA in Tourism & Hospitality Management
Course Title: MSc in Tourism Management & Planning
Course Title: MSc in Tourism Management & Marketing
Course Title: MSc in Tourism & Hospitality Education
Course Title: MSc in Tourism & Environmental Management
Course Title: MA in European Tourism Management

The University of Brighton
Department: Service Sector Management
Course Title: MA/Diploma in Tourism Management

University of Buckingham
Department: History of Art and Heritage Management
Course Title: MA in Heritage and Tourism Management

Buckinghamshire College
Course Title: MSc in Heritage Management and Interpretation
Course Title: MSc in Tourism Development and Management
Course Title: MA in Strategic Leisure Management

Christ Church College Canterbury
Department: Geography
Course Title: MSc in Tourism and Environmental Management

University of Wales Institute, Cardiff
Department: School of Hospitality, Leisure and Tourism
Course Title: MA/PgDip/PgCert in Leisure and Tourism Management

University of Central Lancashire
Department: Hospitality and Tourism
Course Title: MA/PgDip in Tourism, Leisure and Service Management

Cheltenham & Gloucester College of Higher Education
Department: Leisure Management
Course Title: MA/PgDip/PgCert in Leisure and Tourism Management

University of Derby
Course Title: MA/PgCert/PgDip in Tourism Management

Glasgow Caledonian University
Department: Hospitality, Tourism and Leisure Management
Course Title: MPhil/PhD in Hospitality, Tourism and Leisure Management
Course Title: MSc/PgDip/PgCert in Tourism Management

University of Lincolnshire and Humberside
Department: Tourism
Course Title: MA in Tourism Management

Course Title: MA/PgDip/PgCert in Tourism Studies
Course Title: MBA in International Tourism
Course Title: MPhil/PhD in Urban Tourism/Tourism Marketing/
Cultural and Social Tourism/Sustainable Tourism
Department: Information Systems
Course Title: MBA in International Tourism

University of Kent
Department: Anthropology (Durrell Institute of Conservation and
Ecology)
Course Title: MSc in Tourism and Conservation

Lancaster University
Department: Sociology
Course Title: MA in Tourism and Leisure

Liverpool John Moores University
Department: School of Education and Community Studies
Course Title: PgCert in Tourism and Leisure Management

University of Luton
Course Title: MSc in Tourism Management
Course Title: MBA in Tourism Management

Manchester Metropolitan University
Department: Hotel Catering and Tourism Management
Course Title: MPhil/PhD in Hospitality and Tourism Management
Course Title: MSc/PgDip in Tourism Management

Newman College of Higher Education
Course Title: MA/MA (ed)/PgDip/PgCert in Tourism, Management
and the Environment

University of North London
Course Title: MPhil/PhD in Leisure and Tourism
Course Title: MA/PgDip in Leisure and Tourism Studies
Course Title: MA/PgCert in International Tourism Policy
Course Title: MBA in Hospitality and Tourism Management

University of Northumbria at Newcastle
Department: Postgraduate and Postexperience Programmes
Course Title: MA/PgDip in Tourism Management

Oxford Brookes University
Department: School of Planning
Course Title: MSc in Tourism Planning

University of Portsmouth
Department: Land and Construction Management
Course Title: MSc/PgDip/PgCert in Ecotourism

Queen Margaret College
Department: Hospitality and Tourism Management
Course Title: MSc/PgDip in Sustainable Tourism

University College of Ripon and York St John
Department: Sports Science, Leisure and Tourism
Course Title: MA/MPhil/PhD in Sports Science, Leisure and Tourism

Roehampton Institute London
Department: Sociology and Social Policy
Course Title: MA/Graduate Diploma in The Sociology and
Anthropology of Travel and Tourism

Royal Agricultural College
Duration: MA: 1 year full-time
Course Title: MA/PgDip in Rural Recreation and Tourism

Scottish Agricultural College
Department: Leisure and Tourism Management
Course Title: MPhil/PhD in Leisure and Tourism Management

Sheffield Hallam University
Department: Leisure Industries Research Centre
Course Title: MSc/PgDip/PgCert in Tourism Management
Course Title: MPhil/PhD in Environment and Recreational Studies
Course Title: MSc/PgDip/PgCert in International Tourism Management

Staffordshire University
Department: Geographical Division
Course Title: MA in Tourism, Recreation and Environment
Department: Postgraduate Administration
Course Title: MSc/PgDip in Tourism Management

University of Strathclyde
Department: The Scottish Hotel School
Course Title: MSc/PgDip in Tourism

University of Surrey
Department: Management Studies
Course Title: MSc/PgDip in Tourism Management
Course Title: MSc in Tourism Studies
Course Title: MSc/PgDip in Tourism Marketing
Course Title: MSc/PgDip in Tourism Planning and Development

Swansea Institute of Higher Education
Course Title: MSc/PgDip in Tourism and Leisure Resource Management

University of Ulster
Course Title: MA/PgDip in Tourism Management

University of Westminster
Department: Tourism
Course Title: MBA in Tourism

Undergraduate

A significant number of establishments offer undergraduate courses in tourism and related subjects. The following is therefore just an indication of the range on offer.

University of Abertay Dundee
Department: School of Social and Health Sciences
Course Title: BA (Hons) in Tourism

Birmingham College of Food, Tourism and Creative Studies
Course Title: BSc (Hons) in Tourism Management
Course Title: BA (Hons) in Tourism Business Management

The University of Brighton
Department: Service Sector Management
Course Title: BA (Hons) in Tourism Management
Course Title: BA (Hons) in International Tourism Management
Course Title: BA (Hons) in Travel Management

University of the West of England
Course Title: BA/BA (Hons) in European Business Studies with Tourism
Course Title: BA/BA (Hons) in Business Studies with Tourism

Buckinghamshire College
Course Title: BSc (Hons) in Tourism with Marketing
Course Title: BA (Hons) in Travel and Tourism Management
Course Title: BA (Hons) in Tourism with Leisure Management

University of Wales Institute, Cardiff
Department: School of Hospitality, Leisure and Tourism
Course Title: BA (Hons) in Tourism

University of Central England
Department: Business
Duration: 3 years full-time
Course Title: BA (Hons) in Hospitality Management with Tourism

University of Central Lancashire
Course Title: BA (Hons) in Tourism Studies
Course Title: BA (Hons) in Languages with Tourism
Course Title: BA (Hons) in International Tourism

University College Chester
Department: Arts and Humanities
Course Title: BSc (Hons) in Tourism Management

University of Glamorgan
Department: Business School
Course Title: BA (Hons) in Leisure and Tourism Management

Glasgow Caledonian University
Department: Hospitality, Tourism and Leisure Management
Course Title: BA/BA (Hons) in International Travel with Information
Systems

Grimsby College
Department: School of Tourism and Leisure
Course Title: BA (Hons) in Marketing and Tourism Operations

Leeds Metropolitan University
Course Title: BA (Hons) in Tourism Management
Course Title: BA (Hons) in International Tourism Management

University of Lincolnshire
Department: Tourism
Course Title: BA (Hons) in Tourism
Course Title: BA (Hons) in International Tourism
Course Title: BA (Hons) in European Tourism

Liverpool John Moores University
Department: School of Modern Languages/School of Education and
Community Studies
Course Title: BA/BA (Hons) in Tourism and Leisure with a Modern
Language

London College of Printing and Distributive Trades
Department: Professional Studies
Course Title: BA (Hons) in International Travel and Tourism Management

University of Luton
Course Title: BA/BA (Hons) in Travel and Tourism

University of North London
Course Title: BA/BA (Hons) in International Leisure and Tourism
Management
Course Title: BA (Hons) in Leisure and Tourism Management

University of Northumbria
Department: Undergraduate Programmes
Course Title: BA (Hons) in Travel and Tourism
Course Title: BA (Hons) in Travel and Tourism Management

Norwich City College
Department: The Hotel School
Course Title: BA (Hons) in Hospitality and Tourism Management
Course Title: BA (Hons) in Travel and Tourism

University of Plymouth
Course Title: BSc (Hons) in Tourism Management

Queen Margaret College
Course Title: BA (Hons) in Hospitality and Tourism Management
Course Title: BA (Hons) in Tourism Management

Sheffield Hallam University
Course Title: BA (Hons) in Tourism Management

South Bank University
Department Business School Undergraduate
Course Title: BA/BA (Hons) in Modern Languages and International Tourism
Course Title: BA (Hons) in Tourism Management

University of Sunderland
Course Title: BSc (Hons) in Tourism Development Studies

University of Surrey
Course Title: BSc (Hons) in International Hospitality and Tourism Management

University of Westminster
Course Title: BA (Hons) in Business Studies (Services: Travel)
Course Title: BA (Hons) in Tourism and Planning

University of Wolverhampton
Department: Wolverhampton Business School
Course Title: BA/BA (Hons) in Business and Tourism Management

HND and equivalent/Further education

A large number of establishments offer HNC/D courses in tourism and/or management subjects with a tourism option, which vary in duration from one to three years, part or full-time, or sandwich. Similarly, a substantial number have courses leading to, for example, N/SVQs in tourism subjects.

It would be impractical to list them all here. There is bound to be one near where you live, so look in your local *Yellow Pages* and contact them to find out about availability of courses. Alternatively, if you want to find out what is on offer elsewhere, contact the Institute of Travel and Tourism direct.

TRANSPORT (GENERAL AND MISCELLANEOUS)

Postgraduate

University of Wales, Cardiff
Department: City and Regional Planning
Duration: 12 months full-time
Course Title: MSc in Urban and Regional Transport

City University
Department: Shipping, Trade and Finance
Duration: 14 months full-time or 2 years part-time
Course Title: MSc in Shipping, Trade and Finance
Course Title: MSc in Trade, Transport and Finance

Cranfield University
Department: School of Management: Centre for Logistics and Transportation
Duration: MPhil: 1 year full-time or 2 years part-time; PhD: 3 years full-time or 4 years part-time
Course Title: MPhil/PhD in Management Studies (Transport)

Imperial College
Department: Civil Engineering
Duration: DIC: Full-time or part-time; MSc: 12 months full-time or 2 years part-time or 3 years part-time
Course Title: MSc/DIC in Transport

University of Leeds
Duration: MPhil: 2 years full-time or 3 years part-time; PhD: 3 years full-time or 4 years part-time
Course Title: MPhil/PhD in Transport Studies

University of Salford
Department: Geography
Duration: 1 year full-time
Course Title: PgCert in Transport and Development
Department: Management School
Duration: 2 years part-time day and evening
Course Title: MBA in transport

University College London
Department: Civil and Environment Engineering
Duration: 12 months full-time or 2 years part-time or 3 years part-time

Course Title: MSc in Transport
Duration: MPhil: 2 years full-time or 3 years part-time; PhD: 3 years full-time or 5 years part-time
Course Title: MPhil/PhD in Transport

University of Westminster
Department: Transport Studies Group
Course Title: PhD in Transport Studies
Course Title: MSc in Transport Policy: Planning and Management

Undergraduate

Bolton Institute
Department: Mechanical and Automobile Engineering
Duration: 3 to 5 years part-time day and evening or 3 years full-time or 4 years full-time including foundation year
Course Title: BSc (Hons) in Transport Studies
Duration: 3 to 5 years part-time day and evening or 4 years full-time or 5 years full-time including foundation year
Course Title: BSc (Hons) in Transport Studies

University of Central England
Department: School of Planning
Duration: BSc: 3 years full-time; BSc (Hons): 3 years full-time
Course Title: BSc (Hons) in Environmental Planning (Transport and Communication)

Coventry University
Department: Industrial Design
Duration: BA (hons): 3 years full-time or 4 years sandwich; MDes: 4 years full-time or 5 years sandwich
Course Title: BA (Hons)/MDes in Transport Design (Route A)
Course Title: BA (Hons)/MDes in Transport Design (Route B)

University of Huddersfield
Department: Design
Duration: 3 years full-time or 4 years sandwich
Course Title: BA (Hons) in Transport Design (Route A)
Course Title: BA (Hons) in Transport Design (Route B)

Liverpool John Moores University
Department: School of Engineering
Duration: BSc: 3 years full-time or part-time day; BSc (Hons): 3 years full-time or part-time day
Course Title: BSc/BSc (Hons) in Transport

Napier University
Department: Civil and Transportation Engineering
Duration: BSc: 3 years full-time: BSc (Hons): 4 years full-time
Course Title: BSc/BSc (Hons) in Transport Studies
Duration: BSc: 3 years full-time; BSc (Hons): 4 years full-time
Course Title: BSc/BSc (Hons) in Transport Studies with Information
Management

University of Northumbria
Department: Design
Duration: 3 years full-time
Course Title: BA (Hons) in Transportation Design (Route A)
Course Title: BA (Hons) in Transportation Design (Route B)

University of Plymouth
Course Title: BSc (Hons) in Transport

Staffordshire University
Department: Stafford Campus
Duration: 3 years full-time or 4 years sandwich or part-time
Course Title: BSc (Hons) in Transportation Studies
Course Title: BSc (Hons) in Transportation Studies/Management/
Informatics
Duration: 3 years full-time
Course Title: BSc (Hons) in Transport Systems Technology
Duration: 4 years full-time including foundation year or 5 years
sandwich including foundation year
Course Title: BSc (Hons) in Transportation Studies (Extended)
Course Title: BSc (Hons) in Transportation Studies/Management/
Informatics (Extended)
Duration: 4 years full-time including foundation year
Course Title: BSc (Hons) in Transport Systems Technology (Extended)

University of Ulster
Department: Campus: Jordanstown
Duration: 4 years sandwich
Course Title: BSc (Hons) in Transportation

TRANSPORT ADMINISTRATION/ MANAGEMENT (INCL. ECONOMICS)

Postgraduate

Cranfield University
Department: School of Management: Centre for Logistics and Transportation
Duration: MPhil: 1 year full-time or 2 years part-time; PhD: 3 years full-time or 4 years part-time
Course Title: MPhil/PhD in Management Studies (Transport)

University of Huddersfield
Department: Transport and Logistics
Duration: 2 years part-time
Course Title: MSc in Transport and Logistics Management

University of Leeds
Department: Leeds University Business School
Duration: 2 years part-time
Course Title: MBA in Transport Management
Department: Institute for Transport Studies
Duration: MA: 1 year full-time or 2 years part-time/PgDip: 9 months full-time
Course Title: MA/PgDip in Transport Economics

London City College
Course Title: MBA in Maritime Management

University of Newcastle Upon Tyne
Department: Economics
Course Title: MSc in Transport Management and Economics

University of North London
Duration: 1 year full-time or 2 years part-time
Course Title: MA in Transport Policy and Management

University of Salford
Department: Management School
Duration: MSc: 2 years part-time evening; PgDip: 2 years part-time evening
Course Title: MSc/PgDip in Transport and Logistics Management

Sheffield Hallam University
Duration: MA: 1 year full-time or 2 years part-time
Course Title: MA/PgDip/PgCert in Transport Planning and Management

Swansea Institute of Higher Education
Department: Transport
Duration: 1 year full-time or 3 years part-time
Course Title: MSc/PgDip in Transport Planning and Management

University of Westminster
Department: Transport Studies Group
Course Title: MSc in Transport Policy

Undergraduate

Aston University
Department: Civil and Mechanical Engineering
Duration: 3 years full-time/4 years sandwich
Course Title: BSc (Hons) in Transport Management

Loughborough University
Department: Transport Studies
Duration: 3 years full-time/4 years sandwich
Course Title: BSc (Hons) in Transport Management and Planning

North East Wales Institute
Department: Engineering
Duration: 3 years full-time or 4 years part-time
Course Title: BEng (Hons) in Aircraft/Transport Management

Swansea Institute of Higher Education
Department: Transport
Duration: 3 years full-time
Course Title: BSc (Hons) in Transport Management

HND and equivalent

London City College
Duration: 6 months full-time
Course Title: Diploma in Transport Management

Swansea Institute of Higher Education
Department: Transport
Duration: 2 years full-time
Course Title: HND in Transport Management

TRANSPORT ENGINEERING

Postgraduate

University of Birmingham
Department: Civil Engineering
Duration: MSc: 12 months full-time or 2 years part-time; PgDip: 2 years part-time or 8 months full-time
Course Title: MSc/PgDip in International Highway Engineering

University of Leeds
Department: Institute for Transport Studies
Duration: MSc (Eng): 12 months full-time or 24 to 36 months part-time; PgDip: 21 months part-time or 9 months full-time
Course Title: MSc (Eng)/PgDip in Transport Planning and Engineering

Loughborough University
Department: Aeronautical and Automotive Engineering
Duration: MPhil: 12 months full-time or 24 months part-time; PhD 24 months full-time or 33 months part-time
Course Title: MPhil/PhD in Aeronautical and Automotive Engineering

Napier University
Department: Civil and Transportation Engineering
Duration: MSc: 1 year full-time or 2 to 3 years part-time
Course Title: MSc/Pg/Dip in Transportation Engineering
Duration: MPhil: full-time or part-time;PhD: full-time or part-time
Course Title: MPhil/PhD in Civil or Transportation Engineering

University of Newcastle upon Tyne
Department: Civil Engineering
Duration: MPhil: 2 years full-time; PhD: 3 years full-time or 5 years part-time
Course Title: MPhil/PhD in Civil Engineering
Duration: MSc: 1 year full-time; Diploma: 9 months full-time; Certificate: 9 months full-time
Course Title: MSc/Diploma/Certificate in Transport Engineering and Operations

University of Nottingham
Department: Civil Engineering
Duration: 1 year full-time or 2 years part-time or 3 years part-time
Course Title: MSc in Highway Engineering

University of Salford
Department: Civil and Environmental Engineering
Duration: MScs: 1 year full-time or 2 years part-time; PgDip: 2 years
part-time or 8 months full-time
Course Title: MSc/PgDip in Transport Engineering and Planning

Sheffield Hallam University
Duration: MPhil: 3 years full-time or part-time
Course Title: MPhil/PhD in Highway Materials

University of Southampton
Department: Civil and Environmental Engineering
Duration: MSc: 12 months full-time or 2 years part-time
Course Title: MSc/Diploma in Transportation Planning and
Engineering

University of Surrey
Department: Civil Engineering
Duration: MSc: 12 months full-time or 2 to 6 years part-time
Course Title: MSc/PgDip/PgCert in Bridge Engineering

Undergraduate

Doncaster College
Department: Minerals Engineering
Duration: 3 years sandwich
Course Title: BEng in Quarry and Road Surface Engineering

University of Huddersfield
Department: Mechanical and Manufacturing Engineering
Duration: 5 years sandwich
Course Title: MEng in Mechanical and Automotive Design
Course Title: BEng (Hons) in Mechanical and Automotive Design
Duration: 5 years sandwich including foundation year
Course Title: BEng (Hons) in Mechanical and Automotive Design (with
foundation year)

University of Leeds
Department: Civil Engineering
Duration: BEng (Hons): 3 years full-time or 4 years full-time including
foundation year: MEng: 4 years full-time or 5 years full-time including
foundation year
Course Title: BEng (Hons)/MEng in Civil Engineering with Transport
Engineering

Napier University
Department: Civil and Transportation Engineering
Duration: BEng: 3 years full-time; BEng (Hons): 4 years full-time
Course Title: BEng/BEng (Hons) in Civil and Transportation
Engineering

University of Salford
Department: Civil and Environmental Engineering
Duration: 4 years full-time or 5 years sandwich
Course Title: MEng in Civil Engineering with Transport
Duration: 3 years full-time or 4 years sandwich
Course Title: BEng (Hons) in Civil Engineering with Transport

HND and equivalent

City of Bath College
Department: School of Technology
Duration: Distance learning
Course Title: Professional Development Certificate in Civil Engineering
Course Title: Continuing Education Certificate of Achievement in:
Traffic Planning and Engineering
Highway Design
Highway Technology
Highway Materials and Testing
Highway Legislation and Administration
Estimating and Costing: MCDHW
Highway Maintenance

Newham College of Further Education
Department: Construction and the Built Environment
Duration: 2 years part-time day
Course Title: HNC in Civil Engineering and Highways

College of North West London
Department: Automobile, Electronics and Engineering Technology
Duration: 2 years full-time
Course Title: HND in Motor Vehicle Management (Transport
Engineering and Operations)

Further education

City of Bath College
Department: School of Technology
Duration: Distance learning

Course Title: College Award in: Resurfacing and Surface Dressing; Highway Drainage; Public Highways Design and Highways Road Signs and Markings; Ground Investigation; Construction Management Planning; New Roads and Street Works Act; Earthworks for Highways

Belfast Institute of Further and Higher Education
Department: School of Building and Civil Engineering
Duration: 3 years part-time day
Course Title: C&G-614 in Roadwork (Craft and Advanced Craft)

Bishop Auckland College
Department: Technology
Duration: Part-time day
Course Title: C&G-6156 1 in Streetworks Excavation

Leeds College of Building
Department: Advanced Supervision and Management Studies
Duration: Block-release
Course Title: NVQ in Roadworks/Masons Paviour (Levels 1, 2 and 3)

Leicester South Fields College
Department: School of Combined Crafts
Duration: 3 years part-time day
Course Title: C&G-6140 in Roadwork Craft and Advanced Craft
Duration: 1 year part-time day
Course Title: C&G-6230 in Roadwork, Supplementary Studies

Manchester College of Arts and Technology
Duration: 1 year part-time day
Course Title: C&G-623 in Roadwork, Supplementary Studies
Department: Construction
Duration: 2 years part-time day
Course Title: C&G-6140 in Roadwork (Craft and Advanced Craft)

Newham College of Further Education
Education: Construction and the Built Environment
Duration: 2 years part-time day
Course Title: National Certificate in Civil Engineering Studies with Highways and Autocad

Northumberland College
Department: Construction
Duration: various, 1–2 years part-time, evenings, full-time
Course Title: College Award in Highways Construction and Maintenance Training Programme (Advance YT)
Course Title: C&G-6140 in Highway Construction and Maintenance Advanced Craft

Course Title: NVQ in Highways Maintenance (Level 1, 2, 3)
Course Title: C&G-6230 in Roadwork: Highways Construction
(Supplementary Studies)

Omagh College of Further Education
Department: Technology and Science
Duration: 2 years part-time day
Course Title: C&G-614 in Roadwork (Craft)

The Sheffield College
Department: Built Environment
Duration: 1 year full-time
Course Title: C&G-6153/6156 in Highway Maintenance
Duration: 2 years part-time
Course Title: Certificate in Highway Maintenance

Shrewsbury College of Arts
Duration: 2 years part-time day
Course Title: C&G-614 in Roadwork (Craft) (YT)
Course Title: C&G-614 in Roadwork (Craft)

TRANSPORT PLANNING

Postgraduate

University of Leeds
Department: Institute for Transport Studies
Duration: MSc (Eng): 12 months full-time or 24 to 36 months part-time;
PgDip: 21 months part-time or 9 months full-time
Course Title: MSc (Eng)/PgDip in Transport Planning and Engineering

University of Newcastle upon Tyne
Department: Civil Engineering
Duration: MSc: 12 months full-time; Diploma: 9 months full-time
Course Title: MSc/Diploma in Transportation Planning and Policy

Oxford Brookes University
Department: School of Planning
Duration: 12 months full-time or 2 years part-time
Course Title: MSc in Transport Planning

University of Salford
Department: Civil and Environmental Engineering
Duration: MSc: 1 year full-time or 2 years part-time; PgDip: 2 years
part-time or 8 months full-time
Course Title: MSc/PgDip in Transport Engineering and Planning

Sheffield Hallam University
Duration: MA: 1 year full-time or 2 years part-time
Course Title: MA/PgDip/PgCert in Transport Planning and Management

University of Southampton
Department: Civil and Environmental Engineering
Duration: MSc: 12 months full-time or 2 years part-time
Course Title: MSc/Diploma in Transportation Planning and Engineering

Swansea Institute of Higher Education
Department: Transport
Duration: 1 year full-time or 3 years part-time
Course Title: MSc/PgDip in Transport Planning and Management

University of Westminster
Department: Transport Studies Group
Course Title: MSc in Transport Policy: Planning and Management
Duration: MSc: 1 year full-time, or 2 years or 3 years part-time
Course Title: MSc/PgDip in Transport Planning and Management

Undergraduate

Loughborough University
Department: Transport Studies
Duration: 3 years full-time
Course Title: BSc (Hons) in Transport Management and Planning
Duration: 4 years sandwich
Courses Title: BSc (Hons) in Transport Management and Planning

ESTABLISHMENTS

Aberdeen – The Robert Gordon University, Schoolhill, Aberdeen AB10 1FR
Tel: 01224 262207 Fax: 01224 263000
Air Service Training (Engineeering) Ltd, Perth Airport, Perth, Tayside PH2 6NP
Tel: 01738 552311 Fax: 01738 553369
Aston University, Aston Triangle, Birmingham B4 7ET
Tel: 0121 359 3611 Fax: 0121 333 6350
Bath – City of Bath College, Avon Street, Bath, Avon BA1 1UP
Tel: 01225 312191 Fax: 01225 444213

Bath – University of Bath, Claverton Down, Bath, Avon BA2 7AY
Tel: 01225 323019 Fax: 01225 826366
Belfast Institute of Further and Higher Education, Park House, 87–91
Great Victoria Street, Belfast, Northern Ireland BT2 7AG
Tel: 028 90 265000 Fax: 028 90 265451
Berkshire College of Agriculture, Hall Place, Burchetts Green,
Maidenhead, Berkshire SL6 6QR
Tel: 01628 82444 Fax: 01628 824695
Birmingham – University of Birmingham, Edgbaston, Birmingham
B15 2TT
Tel: 0121 414 3344 Fax: 0121 414 7921
Birmingham – University of Central England, Perry Barr,
Birmingham, West Midlands B42 2SU
Tel: 0121 331 5000
Birmingham College of Food, Tourism and Creative Studies, Summer
Row, Birmingham, West Midlands B3 1JB
Tel: 0121 604 1000
Bishop Auckland College, Woodhouse Lane, Bishop Auckland,
County Durham DL14 6JZ
Tel: 01388 603052 Fax: 01388 609294
Bolton College, Manchester Road, Bolton, Lancashire BL2 1ER
Tel: 01204 531411 Fax: 01204 380774
Bolton Institute, Deane Road, Bolton, Lancashire BL3 5AB
Tel: 01204 528851/900600/FREE 0800 262117 Fax: 01204 399074
Bournemouth University, Poole House, Talbot Campus, Fern Barrow,
Poole, Dorset BH12 5BB
Tel: 01202 524111 Fax: 01202 513293
Brighton – The University of Brighton, Mithraw House, Lewes Road,
Brighton, East Sussex BN2 4AT
Bristol – University of the West of England, Frenchay Campus,
Coldharbour Lane, Bristol BS16 1QY
Tel: 0117 965 6261 Fax: 0117 976 3804
Buckingham – University of Buckingham, Buckingham, MK18 1EG
Tel: 01280 814080 Fax: 01280 824081
Buckinghamshire College, Queen Alexandra Road, High Wycombe,
Buckinghamshire HP11 2JZ
Tel: 01494 522141 Fax: 01494 524392
Cardiff – University of Wales, Cardiff, PO Box 494, Cardiff CF1 3YL
Tel 029 20 874404 Fax: 029 20 874130
Cardiff – University of Wales Institute, Cardiff, External Affairs
Department, Central Administration, Western Avenue, Llandaff,
Cardiff CF5 2SG
Tel: 029 20 506070 Fax: 029 20 506911

Castlereach College of Further Education, Montgomery Road, Belfast, Northern Ireland BT6 9JD
Tel: 028 90 797144 Fax: 028 90 401820
Central Lancashire – University of Central Lancashire, Preston, Lancashire PR1 2HE
Tel: 01772 201201 Fax: 01772 892946
Cheltenham & Gloucester College of Higher Education, PO Box 220, The Park, Cheltenham, Gloucester GL50 2QF
Tel: 01242 532825 Fax: 01242 256759
Chester – University College, Cheyney Road, Chester, Cheshire CH1 4BJ
Tel: 01244 375444 Fax: 01244 373379
Christ Church College, North Holmes Road, Canterbury, Kent CT1 1QU
Tel: 01227 767700 Fax: 01227 470442
Cornwall College, Trevenson Road, Redruth, Cornwall TR15 3RD
Tel: 01209 712911 Fax: 01209 713338
Coventry University, Priory Street, Coventry, West Midlands CV1 5FB
Tel: 024 76 631313 Fax: 024 76 838793
Cranfield University, Cranfield Campus, Cranfield, Bedford MK43 OAL
(See also Cranfield: Silsoe Campus, Shrivenham Campus)
Tel: 01234 750111 Fax: 01234 750875
Derby – University of Derby, Kedleston Road, Derby, Derbyshire DE3 1GB
Tel: 01332 622222 Fax: 01332 294861
Doncaster College, Waterdale, Doncaster, South Yorkshire DN1 3EX
Tel: 01302 553553 Fax: 01302 553559
Dundee – University of Abertay Dundee, Bell Street, Dundee D1 1HG
Tel: 01382 308000 Fax: 01382 308877
East London – University of East London, Barking Campus, Longbridge Road, Dagenham, Essex RM8 2AS
Stratford Campus, Romford Road, London E15 4LZ
Tel: 020 8590 7722/7000 Fax: 020 8590 7799
East Surrey College, Gatton Point, Claremont Road, Redhill, Surrey RH1 2JX
Tel: 01737 772611 Fax: 01737 768641
Eastleigh College, Chestnut Avenue, Eastleigh, Hampshire SO50 5HT
Tel: 023 80 326326 Fax: 023 80 620654
Edinburgh – Heriot-Watt University, Admissions Office, Riccarton, Edinburgh EH14 4AS
(See also Edinburgh College of Art, Moray House, Institute of Education, Scottish College of Textiles)
Tel: 0131 449 5111 Fax: 0131 449 5153

Edinburgh – Queen Margaret College, Admissions Office, Clerwood Terrace, Edinburgh EH12 8TS
Tel: 0131 317 3000 Fax: 0131 317 3256
Edinburgh – University of Edinburgh, Secretary's Office, Old College, South Bridge, Edinburgh
Tel: 0131 650 1000 Fax: 0131 650 2147
Glamorgan – University of Glamorgan, Llantwit Road, Treforest, Pontypridd, Mid Glamorgan CF37 1DL
Tel: 01443 480480 Fax: 01443 480558
Glasgow – University of Glasgow, Glasgow G12 8QQ
Tel: 0141 339 8855 Fax: 0141 330 4920
Glasgow – University of Strathclyde, McCance Building, 16 Richmond Street, Glasgow G1 1XQ
Tel: 0141 552 4400 Fax: 0141 552 0775
Glasgow Caledonian University, Cowcaddens Road, Glasgow G4 OBA
Tel: 0141 331 3000 Fax: 0141 331 3005
Glasgow College of Nautical Studies, 21 Thistle Street, Glasgow G5 9XB
Tel: 0141 565 2500 Fax: 0141 565 2599
Grimsby College, Nuns Corner, Grimsby, North East Lincolnshire DN34 5BQ
Tel: 01472 311222 Fax: 01472 879924
Guildford – University of Surrey, Guildford, Surrey GU2 5XH
Tel: 01483 300800 Fax: 01483 300803
Hertfordshire – University of Hertfordshire, College Lane, Hatfield, Hertfordshire AL10 9AB
Tel: 01707 284000 Fax: 01707 284738
Huddersfield – University of Huddersfield, Queensgate, Huddersfield, West Yorkshire HD1 3DH
Tel: 01484 422288 Fax: 01484 516151
Hull – University of Hull, Cottingham Road, Hull, North Humberside HU6 7RX
Tel: 01482 46311 Fax: 01482 442290
Imperial College, London SW7 2AZ
Tel: 0171 589 5111 Fax: 0171 594 8004
Kent – University of Kent, Canterbury, Kent CT2 7NZ
Tel: 01227 764000 Fax: 01227 452196
Lancaster University, Bailrigg, Lancaster, Lancashire LA1 4YW
Tel: 01524 65201 Fax: 01524 846243
Leeds – University of Leeds, Leeds, West Yorkshire LS2 9JT
Tel: 0113 233 2332 Fax: 0113 233 2334
Leeds College of Building, North Street, Leeds, West Yorkshire LS2 7QT
Tel: 0113 222 600 Fax: 0113 222 6001

Leeds Metropolitan University, Calverley Street, Leeds, West Yorkshire
LS1 3HE
Tel: 0113 283 2600 Fax: 0113 283 3114
Leicester – University of Leicester, Unviersity Road, Leicester,
Leicestershire LE1 7RH
Tel: 0116 252 2522 (Switchboard) 0116 252 2294 (Admissions)
Fax: 0116 252 2447 (Admissions) 0116 252 2200 (General)
Leicester South Fields College, Aylestone Road, Leicester, LE2 7LW
Tel: 0116 254 1818 Fax: 0116 265 3147
**Lincolnshire and Humberside – University of Lincolnshire and
Humberside**, Humberside University Campus, Cottingham Road,
Hull, North Humberside HU6 7RT
Tel: 01482 440550 ext 3230 Fax: 01482 463310
Liverpool – University of Liverpool, Liverpool L69 3BX
Tel: 0151 794 2000 Fax: 0151 708 6502
Liverpool John Moores University, Rodney House, 70 Mount Pleasant,
Liverpool, Merseyside L3 5UX
Tel: 0151 231 5090/5091 Fax: 0151 231 3194
London – City University, Northampton Square, London EC1V OHB
Tel: 020 7477 8000 Fax: 020 7477 8560
London – City of Westminster College, 25 Paddington Green, London
W2 1NB
Tel: 020 7723 8826 Fax: 020 7258 2747
London – University College, Gower Street, London WC1E 6BT
Tel: 020 7380 7365 Fax: 020 7380 7380
London – University of North London, 166–220 Holloway Road,
London N7 8DB
Tel: 020 7607 2789 Fax: 020 7753 5075
London – University of Westminster, 309 Regent Street, London W1R
8AL
Tel: 020 7911 5000 Fax: 020 7911 5788
London City College, Royal Waterloo House, 51–55 Waterloo Road,
London SE1 8TX
Tel: 020 7928 0029/0938/0901 Fax: 020 7401 2231
London College of Printing and Distributive Trades, Elephant and
Castle, London SE1 6SB
Tel: 020 7514 6540 Fax: 020 7514 6535
London Guildhall University, 31 Jewry Street, London EC3N 2EY
Tel: 020 7320 1000 Fax: 020 7320 3462
Loughborough University, Loughborough, Leicestershire LE11 3TU
Tel: 01509 263171
Luton – University of Luton, Park Square, Luton, Bedfordshire LU1 3JU
Tel: 01582 34111 Fax: 01582 418677

Macclesfield College, Park Lane, Macclesfield, Cheshire SK11 8LF
Tel: 01625 427744 Fax: 01625 501084
Manchester College of Arts and Technology, City Centre Campus,
Lower Hardman Street, Manchester, Greater Manchester M3 3ER
Tel: 0161 953 2263 Fax: 0161 953 2259
Manchester Metropolitan University, All Saints, Manchester M15 6BH
Tel: 0161 247 2000 Fax: 0161 236 6390
Middlesex University, Tottenham, White Hart Lane, London N17 8HR
Tel: 020 8362 5000 Fax: 020 8362 5649
Milton Keynes College, Chaffron Way, West Leadenhall, Milton
Keynes, Buckinghamshire MK6 5LP
Tel: 01908 684444 Fax: 01908 684399
Morley College, 61 Westminster Bridge Road, London SE1 7HT
Tel: 020 7928 8501 Fax: 020 7928 4074
Motherwell College, Dalzell Drive, Motherwell, Lanarkshire ML1 2DD
Tel: 01698 232323 Fax: 01698 275430
Napier University, 219 Colinton Road, Edinburgh EH14 1DJ
Tel: 0131 444 2266 Fax: 0131 455 4666
Newcastle upon Tyne – University of Newcastle upon Tyne,
Newcastle upon Tyne, Tyne & Wear NE1 7RU
Tel: 0191 222 6000 Fax: 0191 222 6139
Newcastle upon Tyne – University of Northumbria, Ellison Building,
Ellison Place, Newcastle upon Tyne, Tyne & Wear NE1 8ST
Tel: 0191 227 4064 Fax: 0191 227 4017
Newham College of Further Education, High Street South, London E6
4ER
Tel: 020 8257 4000 Fax: 020 8257 4325
Newman College of Higher Education, Genners Lane, Bartley Green,
Birmingham, West Midlands B32 3NT
Tel: 0121 476 1181 Fax: 0121 476 1196
North Atlantic Fisheries College, Port Arthur, Scalloway, Shetland ZE1
OUN
Tel: 01595 880328 Fax: 01595 880549
North West Kent College, Miskin Road, Dartford, Kent DA1 2LU
Tel: 01322 225471 Fax: 01322 229460
North West London – College of North West London, Dudden Hill
Lane, Denzil Road, London NW10 2XD
Tel: 020 8208 5000 Fax: 020 8208 5151
Northumberland College, College Road, Ashington, Northumberland
NE26 9RG
Tel: 01670 841200 Fax: 01670 841201
Norwich City College, Ipswich Road, Norwich, Norfolk NR2 2LJ
Tel: 01603 773300 Fax: 01603 773301

Nottingham – University of Nottingham, University Park, Nottingham, Nottinghamshire NG7 2RD
Tel: 0115 951 5756 Fax: 0115 951 5795
Nottingham Trent University, Burton Street, Nottingham NG1 4BU
Tel: 0115 941 8418 Fax: 0115 948 4266
Omagh College of Further Education, Omagh, County Tyrone, Northern Ireland BT79 7AH
Tel: 01662 245433
Open Learning Centre International, 24 King Street, Carmarthen SA31 1BS
Tel: 01267 235268 Fax: 01267 238179
Oxford Air Training School, Oxford Airport, Kidlington, Oxford OX5 1RA
Tel: 01865 841234 Fax: 01865 378797
Oxford Brookes University, Gipsy Lane, Headington, Oxford OX3 OBP
Tel: 01865 741111 Fax: 01865 483073
Oxford College of Further Education, Oxpens Road, Oxford, Oxfordshire OX1 1SA
Tel: 01865 245871 Fax: 01865 248871
Petroleum & Energy Studies College, Sun Alliance House, New Inn, Hall Street, Oxford OX1 2QD
Tel: 01865 250521 Fax: 01865 791474
Plymouth – University of Plymouth, Drake Circus, Plymouth, Devon PL4 8AA
Tel: 01752 600600 Fax: 01752 232141
Portsmouth – University of Portsmouth, Winston Churchill Avenue, Portsmouth, Hampshire PO1 2UP
Tel: 023 92 876543 Fax: 023 92 842082
Ripon and York – University College, Lord Mayor's Walk, York, North Yorkshire YO31 7EX
Tel: 01904 656771 Fax: 01904 612512
Roehampton Institute London, Senate House, Roehampton Lane, London SW15 5PU
Tel: 020 8392 3000 Fax: 020 8392 3131
Royal Agricultural College, Stroud Road, Cirencester, Gloucestershire GL7 6JS
Tel: 01285 652531 Fax: 01285 641282
Salford – University of Salford, The Crescent, Salford, Manchester M5 4WT
Tel: 0161 295 5000 Fax: 0161 295 5999
Salisbury College, Southampton Road, Salisbury, Wiltshire SP1 2LW
Tel: 01722 323711 Fax: 01722 326006

ـ sh .ncruive, Ayr, Strathclyde KA6 5H.v
(see also Scoﬁ .llege Aberdeen, Scottish Agricultural College, Edi

Tel: 01292 520 525349
Sheffield College .ie), Granville Road, Sheffield, South Yorkshire S2 2RL
Tel: 0114 260 2100 Fax: 0114 260 2101
Sheffield Hallam University, Pond Street, Sheffield, South Yorkshire S1 1WB
Tel: 0114 272 0911 Fax: 0114 253 2159
Sheffield – The University, 14 Favell Road, Sheffield S3 7QX
Tel: 0114 276 8555 Fax: 0114 276 8014
Shrewsbury College of Arts and Technology, London Road, Shrewsbury, Shropshire SY2 6PR
Tel: 01743 231544 Fax: 01743 241684
South Bank University, 103 Borough Road, London SE1 OAA
Tel: 020 7928 8989 Fax: 020 7815 8158
South Birmingham College, Cole Bank Road, Birmingham, West Midlands B28 8ES
Tel: 0121 694 5000 Fax: 0121 694 5007
South Tyneside College, St George's Avenue, South Shields, Tyne & Wear NE34 6ET
Tel: 0191 427 3500 Fax: 0191 427 3535
Southampton – University of Southampton, Highfield, Southampton, Hampshire SO17 1BJ
Tel: 023 80 595000 Fax: 023 80 593037
Southampton City College, St Mary Street, Southampton, Hampshire SO14 1AR
Tel: 023 80 577400 Fax: 023 80 636728
Southampton Institute, East Park Terrace, Southampton, Hampshire SO14 OYN
Tel: 023 80 319000 Fax: 023 80 222259
Southport College, Mornington Road, Southport, Merseyside PR9 0TT
Tel: 01704 500606 Fax: 01704 546240
St Andrews – The University of St Andrew's, College Gate, St Andrews, Fife KY16 9AJ
Tel: 01334 476161 Fax: 01334 463388
Staffordshire University, College Road, Stoke-on-Trent ST4 2DE
Tel: 01782 294000 Fax: 01782 745422
Stoke-on-Trent College, Cauldon Campus, Stoke Road, Shelton, Stoke-on-Trent, Staffordshire ST4 2DG
Tel: 01782 208208 Fax: 01782 603504

Sunderland – University of Sunderland, Langham To...., Ryhope
Road, Sunderland, Tyne & Wear SR2 7EE
Tel: 0191 515 3000 Fax: 0191 515 3805
Swansea Institute of Higher Education, Townhill, Swansea SA2 OUT
Tel: 01792 481010 Fax: 01792 481085
Tameside College, Beaufort Road, Ashton under Lyne, Lancashire OL6
6NX
Tel: 0161 330 6911/1830 Fax: 0161 343 2738
Teesside Tertiary College, Marton Campus, Marton Road,
Middlesbrough, Cleveland TS4 3RZ
Tel: 01642 300100 Fax: 01642 300893
University of Ulster, Northland Road, Londonderry BT48 7JL
Tel: 01504 371371 Fax: 01504 375410
West Cumbria College, Park Lane, Workington, Cumbria CA14 2RW
Tel: 01900 64331
West Suffolk College, Out Risbygate, Bury St Edminds, Suffolk IP33
3RL
Tel: 01284 701301 Fax: 01284 750561
Wolverhampton – University of Wolverhampton, Molineux Street,
Wolverhampton, West Midlands WV1 1SB
Tel: 01902 321000
York – University of York, Heslington, York, North Yorkshire Y01 5DD
Tel: 01904 430000 Fax: 01904 433433/Admissions 01904 433538

TRANSPORT VOCATIONAL TRAINING AND QUALIFICATIONS

There are now real opportunities to leave full-time education and learn to do a job, gaining experience and qualifications as you go.

Training for management

You will have noticed throughout this guide that many employers offer management/graduate training schemes.

The principle behind these training schemes is the need to prepare dynamic and well-motivated individuals, who are committed to a career in their chosen sector of the industry, for the special responsibilities and demands of management. Candidates therefore also need to possess, or show the ability to develop, the particular qualities and skills they will need.

The in-company schemes are combinations of hands-on learning and more formalised interactive training.

Modern Apprenticeships

Modern Apprenticeships are mainly for well-motivated school and college leavers who have the ability to attain high levels of skills and qualifications. They offer the prospect of top-quality employer-based training leading to nationally recognised qualifications at N/SVQ (see below) Level 3 or above. While the standards to be attained are set, the Modern Apprenticeships are flexible, with the training programme and career routes being adapted to the particular company's commercial and technical needs and the individual employee's aspirations.

The scheme is supported locally by a range of LEC/TECs who work with employers to develop the training to meet the company's needs. Selection of the employees is the responsibility of the company involved and the apprentice is, wherever possible, given employed status at the start of training.

For more information on the Modern Apprenticeship schemes in the transport sector of your choice, contact your LEC/TEC or local careers advisory service.

Transport and N/SVQs

You may be a non-manager, for example an operator or administrator, a specialist in a particular function, a manager or an apprentice. Whichever you are, it is also certain that there will be an N/SVQ applicable to you. There are five levels which can lead to accreditation at the moment.

There are many benefits to the system, which are as relevant and applicable in the transport industry as in any other. Competent performance is recognised through a national qualification and your horizons are widened as a result. The achievement of competence, and its recognition, is motivating, enhancing job satisfaction and heightening job involvement.

Your performance improves and you can gain assistance where you identify it is needed. You know what standards are expected and how you will be assessed, and examinations are not normally required. There are no failures; 'not yet up to standard' simply points to where improvements can be made.

As N/SVQs are made up of a number of units, each of which may be accredited separately, you do not have to work towards a complete qualification all at once. You can be assessed for a single unit, or a cluster of related units, for which you will receive a certificate of unit accreditation. By accumulating certificates you can eventually achieve a complete N/SVQ, or you can select units from a number of different N/SVQs to produce a personal profile of competence which completely describes your ability. N/SVQs thus increase your marketability; a well-presented portfolio of certificates confirming competence can help if you need to get another job. Evidence of competence is also useful at appraisal time.

If you are already employed, the first enquiry should be made to your employer. More and more employers are recognising that they can gain a competitive edge by having competent staff; many are encouraging their staff to gain recognition for this competence and helping them to do so.

If you are not employed, or your employer is not yet aware of the benefits of N/SVQs, you can approach any of the following:

◼ an awarding body (ie one which accredits the qualifications you require, for example OUVS/TVG; see below);
◼ your local college of further education;
◼ an industry national training organisation;
◼ your nearest LEC/TEC.

For transport N/SVQs, the awarding bodies are as follows:

AITT	Association of Industrial Truck Trainers, Huntingdon House, 87 Market Street, Ashby-de-la-Zouch, Leics LE65 1AH (tel: 01530 417234)
AMD	Automotive Management and Development, Regency House, 34 High Street, Rickmansworth, Herts WD3 1ET (tel: 01923 896607)
ATA	Aviation Training Association, 125 London Road, High Wycombe, Bucks HP11 1BT (tel: 01494 445262)
BTEC	Business and Technology Education Council, EDEXCEL Foundation, 32 Russell Square, London WC1B 5DN (tel: 020 7393 4500)
CG	City & Guilds of London Institute, 1 Giltspur Street, London EC1A 9DD (tel: 020 7294 2468)
CITB	Construction Industry Training Boards, Bircham Newton, Near Kings Lynn, Norfolk PE31 6RH (tel: 01553 776677)
DOSC	Distributive Occupational Standards Council, The Coda Centre, 189 Munster Road, London SW6 6AW (tel: 020 7386 5599)

EMTA/EAL	Engineering and Marine Training Authority Awards Ltd/Engineering Awards Ltd, 41 Clarendon Road, Watford WD1 1HS (tel: 01923 238441)
IMI	The Institute of the Motor Industry, Fanshaws, Brickendon, Herts SG13 8PQ (tel: 01992 511521)
LCCI	London Chamber of Commerce and Industry Examinations Board, 112 Station Road, Sidcup, Kent DA15 7BJ (tel: 020 8302 0261)
LGMB	Local Government Management Board, Layden House, 78–86 Turnmill Street, London EC1M 5QU (tel: 020 7296 6600)
MODEF	Ministry of Defence, CM(s), 2BIVT, Room 2307, Kentigern House, 65 Brown Street, Glasgow G2 8EX (tel: 0141 224 2517)
NEBSM	National Examining Board for Supervision & Management, 1 Giltspur Street, London EC1A 9DD (tel: 020 7294 2470)
NPTC	National Proficiency Tests Council, National Agriculture Centre, Stoneleigh, Kenilworth, Warwickshire CV8 2LG (tel: 01203 696553)
OU	The Open University, Validation Services, 344–354 Gray's Inn Road, London WC1X 8BP (tel: 020 7278 4411)
QFI	Qualifications for Industry Ltd, 80 Richardshaw Lane, Pudsey, Leeds LS28 6BN (tel: 0113 239 3355)
RHDTC	Road Haulage and Distribution Training Council, 14 Warren Yard, Wolverton Mill, Milton Keynes MK12 5NW (tel: 01908 313360)
RITC	Rail Industry Training Council, Africa House, 64/78 Kingsway, London WC2B 6AH (tel: 020 7320 0436)
RSA	RSA Examinations Board, Westwood Way, Coventry CV4 8HS (tel: 01203 470033)
TVG	Transportation Vocational Group, 80 Portland Place, London W1N 4DP (tel: 020 7467 9400)

Current NVQs

Title	Level	Awarding body
Cargo operations	1, 2	BTEC
Coordinating airside ramp operations	3	ATA
Controlling air terminal operations	3, 4	ATA
Controlling aircraft operations	3, 4	ATA
Controlling airport operations	3, 4	ATA

Distribution and warehousing	3	IMI-DOSC
operations	2	BTEC-DOSC, CG-DOSC, CG-RHDTC, EMTA/EAL, EMTA/EAL, MODEF, IMI-DOSC, LCCI, QFI-DOSC, RSA- DOSC
	3	BTEC-DOSC, CG-DOSC, EMTA/EAL, DOSC, RSA-DOSC
	4	BTEC-DOSC, CG-DOSC
Distributive operations	1	BTEC-DOSC, CG-DOSC, EMTA/EAL, EMTA/EAL-MODEF, IMI-DOSC, LCCI, QFI-DOSC, RSA-DOSC
Driving instruction	3	AMD
Fishing vessel operations	3, 4	BTEC
Handling air passengers	2, 3	ATA
Highways maintenance	1, 2, 3	CG-LGMB
	4	OU-TVG
Lift truck operations	2	AITT, CG, CITB-CG, EMTA-EAL, RSA
Maintaining automotive vehicles	1, 2	AMD
body structures and claddings	3	AMD
electrical/electronic	3	AMD
mechanical	3	AMD
Marine – fishing vessel engineering	2, 4	BTEC
Marine operations:		
harbour-based	2	BTEC
shore-based	1	BTEC
Merchant vessel operations	2, 3, 4	BTEC
Piloting transport aircraft	3	EMTA/ELA
Piloting transport aircraft	4	EMTA/ELA
Planning aircraft payloads	3	ATA
Port passenger operations	2	BTEC
Providing air cargo booking and airway-billing services	3	ATA

Providing air passenger ticketing services	2, 3	ATA
Providing airside ramp services	2	ATA
Rail transport:		
signal operations	2	CG-RITC
driving	2	CG-RITC
passenger service	2	CG-RITC
shunting	2	CG-RITC
Rail control room operations	3	CG-RITC
Rail transport engineering maintenance:		
communications	2, 3	CG-RITC
electrification	2, 3	CG-RITC
permanent way	2, 3	CG-RITC
plant	2, 3	CG-RITC
signal fault finding	2, 3	CG-RITC
signals	2, 3	CG-RITC
traction and rolling stock	2, 3	CG-RITC
Road transport:		
assisting in road haulage and distribution operations	1	RHDTC
transporting goods by road	2	RHDTC
organising road transport operations	2	RHDTC
distribution and warehousing operations	2	RHDTC
road haulage and distribution operations	3	RHDTC
Tourist information	2, 3	RSA
Traffic management and systems engineering	4	OU-TVG
Transport planning	5	OU-TVG
Transporting passengers by road:		
long itineraries	3	AMD
passenger support services	2	AMD
short itineraries	2	AMD
Travel services	2, 3	BTEC, CG, RSA
commentaries and interpretation for tourism	2, 3	BTEC, CG, RSA
leisure and business travel	4	BTEC
leisure and business	4	CG
supervising	3	BTEC, CG
tour operations	2, 3	BTEC, CG, RAS
	4	BTEC, CG

Vehicle maintenance – service replacement	1, 2	BTEC, CG, IMI, RSA
Vehicle parts distribution and supply	1, 2, 3	BTEC, CG, RSA
Vehicle valeting	1	BTEC, CG, IMI, RSA

Current GNVQs

Leisure and tourism	F, I, A	EDEXCEL (BTEC), CG, RSA
Retail and distributive services	I, A	EDEXCEL (BTEC), CG, RSA

Key: F = Foundation; I = Intermediate; A = Advanced

Future NVQs

It is hoped that the following will also be available soon:

Air Transport
(contact ATA for further details, awards made by EMTA/ELA)
Piloting Rotary Wing Transport Aircraft Level 3
Piloting Rotary Wing Transport Aircraft Level 4

Ports
(contact British Ports Industry Training Ltd for details 01284 811555, awards made by BTEC)
Port Supervisory Management – Marine Level 3
Port Supervisory Management – Cargo Handling Level 3
Port Supervisory Management – Passenger Handling Level 3

Rail Transport
(contact RITC for further information)
Railway Engineering Renewals and Installation:
Permanent Way Level 2
Permanent Way Level 3
Signals Level 2
Signals Level 3
Communications Level 2
Communications Level 3
Electrification Level 2
Electrification Level 3

Rail Control Room Operations Level 2
Train Servicing Level 2
Railway Site Works Control Level 2

Various
(contact OU or TVG for details)
Car Parking Management Levels 3 and 4
Transport Planning Level 4
Transport Technical Support Level 3
Town Planning Support Level 3

Appendix 2: Statistical Profiles

The following tables provide a picture of the transport industry in statistical terms, and are worth careful study since they dispose of a number of common misconceptions. The source is the annual *Transport Statistics Great Britain*, 1998 edition, published by the Government Statistical Service.

Table 2.1 Passengers carried, by mode of transport, 1997

Mode of transport	Carryings (billion passenger kilometres)	Percentage
ROAD		
Buses and coaches	43	6
Cars, vans and taxis	619	86
Motor cycles	4	1
Pedal cycles	4	1
All road	670	93
RAIL and LRT	41	6
AIR (internal)	6.8	0.9
All modes	717	100

Note – LRT = 'Light Rapid Transit' (listed as Urban Rail)
Totals may not add up exactly due to rounding

Table 2.2 Transport casualty rates, by mode, average 1996

Mode of transport	Casualty rate (per billion passenger kilometres)	
	Killed or seriously injured	All severities
AIR	0	–
RAIL	0.3	19
ROAD		
Bus and coach	14	194
Car	42	356
Van	17	125
Two-wheeled motor vehicles	1391	5176
Pedal cycle	880	5706
PEDESTRIAN	633	2528

Table 2.3 Goods carried, by mode of transport, 1997

Mode of transport	Goods lifted		Goods moved	
	(million tonnes)	(percentage)	(billion tonne kilometres)	(percentage)
ROAD	1740	81	157.1	67
RAIL	105	5	16.9	7
WATER	143	7	48.2	21
PIPELINE	148	7	11.2	5
All modes	2136	100	233.4	100

Table 2.4 Household expenditure on transport, 1997

	£ per week
All motoring expenditure	41.20
Rail and tube fares	1.29
Bus and coach fares	1.38
Air fares*	0.74
Other transport and travel	2.26
All transport and travel	46.87
All household expenditure	309.07
Percentage of household expenditure on transport and travel	15.7%

* Excludes air fare component of package holidays abroad

Table 2.5 Households with regular use of cars, 1995–97

Area type	Percentage of households			
	No car	One car	Two cars	Three or more cars
London	40	43	14	2
Metropolitan areas	42	40	16	3
Other urban areas, population over				
250,000	34	45	18	3
25,000 to 250,000	30	46	20	3
3,000 to 25,000	22	47	27	4
Rural areas	16	46	31	8
All areas	31	45	21	4

Table 2.6 Number of UK-owned trading vessels of 500 gross tonnes and over, 1997 (end of year)

Type of vessel	Numbers
Tankers	123
Bulk carriers	35
Specialised carriers	11
Fully cellular container	60
Ro-Ro (passenger and cargo)	85
Other general cargo	156
Passenger	16
Total	486
Of which – UK and Crown	
Dependency registered	392

Table 2.7 Traffic at United Kingdom airports, 1997

Category	Thousands of landings or take-offs
INTERNATIONAL (1)	
UK Operators	
Scheduled	397
Non-scheduled	217
Total	614
Foreign Operators	
Scheduled	413
Non-scheduled	54
Total	467
DOMESTIC (2)	
Scheduled	292
Non-scheduled	49
Total	341
UK OPERATORS TOTAL (2)	
Scheduled	689
Non-scheduled	266
Total	955
OTHER OPERATORS	467
ALL OPERATORS (2)	1423
of which – (3)	
Gatwick	230
Heathrow	431
Luton	40
Stansted	84
Birmingham	80
East Midlands	41
Manchester	147
Newcastle	42
Aberdeen	87
Edinburgh	72
Glasgow	82
Belfast	35

Notes: (1) Includes traffic to/from UK oil rigs
      (2) Adjusted to eliminate double counting
      (3) Includes double counting

Further Reading

While every attempt has been made to limit the list to books believed to be in print at the time of compilation, it has been necessary to include a number of titles no longer available other than in libraries. The majority of the titles listed will be found in the Library of the Institute of Logistics and Transport.

1. General background

Barker, T and Gerhold, D (1995) *The Rise and Rise of Road Transport 1700–1990*, Cambridge University Press, Cambridge

Faulks, R W (1999) *International Transport: An introduction*, Kogan Page, London

Glaister, S *et al* (1998) *Transport Policy in Britain*, Macmillan, London

Gubbins, E J (1998) *Managing Transport Operations*, 2nd edn, Kogan Page, London

Shaw, S J (1993) *Transport: Strategy and policy*, Blackwell, Oxford

Tolley, R S and Turton, B J (1995) *Transport Systems, Policy and Planning*, Longman, Harlow

2. Economics

Bamford, C (1995) *Transport Economics*, Heinemann, Oxford

Burton, K (1993) *Transport Economics*, 2nd edn, Edward Elgar, Cheltenham

Cole, S (1998) *Applied Transport Economics*, 2nd edn, Kogan Page, London

3. Air transport and airports

Ashford, N *et al* (1995) *Airport Operations*, Pitman, London

Doganis, R (1992) *Flying Off Course: The economics of air transport*, Routledge, London

Hanlon, P (1995) *Global Airlines*, Heinemann, Oxford

Shaw, S J (1990) *Airline Marketing and Management*, Pitman, London

4. Sea transport

Alderton, P (1995) *Sea Transport: Operation and economics*, Thomas Reed, East Molesey

Branch, A (1996) *Elements of Shipping*, Chapman & Hall, London

Branch, A (1998) *Maritime Economics: Management and marketing*, Stanley Thornes, Cheltenham

5. The movement of goods

Benson, D (1994) *Elements of Road Transport Management*, Croner, Kingston upon Thames

Lowe, D (1998) *The European Road Freighting Handbook*, Kogan Page, London

Lowe, D (1999) *The Transport Manager's and Operator's Handbook*, 29th edn, Kogan Page, London

6. Passenger transport

Harris, N (1992) *Planning Passenger Railways*, Transport Publishing Company, Glossop

Hibbs, J (1989) *Marketing Management in the Bus and Coach Industry*, Croner, Kingston upon Thames

Lowe, D (1995) *The European Bus and Coach Handbook*, Kogan Page, London

White, P (1995) *Public Transport: Its planning, management and operation*, 3rd edn, UCL Press, London

7. Logistics and distribution management

Christopher, M (1992) *Logistics and Supply Chain Management*, Pitman, London

Cooper, J (1993) *Strategy Planning in Logistics and Transportation*, Cranfield, Bedford

Fawcett, P (1992) *Logistics Management*, Pitman, London

Ruston, A and Oxley, J (1991) *Handbook of Logistics and Distribution Management*, Kogan Page, London

Waters, D (ed) (1999) *Global Logistics and Distribution Planning: Strategies for management*, 3rd edn, Kogan Page, London

8. A selection of periodicals

Bus & Coach Professional (monthly)

Coach & Bus Week (weekly)

Commercial Motor (weekly)

Distribution Business (monthly)

Fairplay (shipping) (weekly)

Flight International (weekly)

Freight (monthly)

Local Transport Today (fortnightly)

Logistics & Transport Focus (monthly)

Modern Railways (monthly)

Motor Transport (weekly)

Railway Gazette International (monthly)

Traffic Engineering & Control (monthly)

Transit (fortnightly)

The author's thanks are due to Karen Isaksen, Librarian, Institute of Logistics and Transport, for help in compiling this listing. Any glaring omissions remain the author's responsibility.

Index